Lecture Notes in Computer Science 11515

Commenced Publication in 1973
Founding and Former Series Editors:
Gerhard Goos, Juris Hartmanis, and Jan van Leeuwen

Editorial Board Members

David Hutchison
  Lancaster University, Lancaster, UK
Takeo Kanade
  Carnegie Mellon University, Pittsburgh, PA, USA
Josef Kittler
  University of Surrey, Guildford, UK
Jon M. Kleinberg
  Cornell University, Ithaca, NY, USA
Friedemann Mattern
  ETH Zurich, Zurich, Switzerland
John C. Mitchell
  Stanford University, Stanford, CA, USA
Moni Naor
  Weizmann Institute of Science, Rehovot, Israel
C. Pandu Rangan
  Indian Institute of Technology Madras, Chennai, India
Bernhard Steffen
  TU Dortmund University, Dortmund, Germany
Demetri Terzopoulos
  University of California, Los Angeles, CA, USA
Doug Tygar
  University of California, Berkeley, CA, USA

More information about this series at http://www.springer.com/series/7408

Joao Eduardo Ferreira · Aibek Musaev ·
Liang-Jie Zhang (Eds.)

Services Computing – SCC 2019

16th International Conference
Held as Part of the Services Conference Federation, SCF 2019
San Diego, CA, USA, June 25–30, 2019
Proceedings

 Springer

Editors
Joao Eduardo Ferreira ⓘ
University of Sao Paulo
São Paulo, Brazil

Aibek Musaev ⓘ
The University of Alabama
Tuscaloosa, AL, USA

Liang-Jie Zhang ⓘ
Kingdee International Software Group
Co., Ltd.
Shenzhen, China

ISSN 0302-9743   ISSN 1611-3349   (electronic)
Lecture Notes in Computer Science
ISBN 978-3-030-23553-6   ISBN 978-3-030-23554-3   (eBook)
https://doi.org/10.1007/978-3-030-23554-3

LNCS Sublibrary: SL2 – Programming and Software Engineering

This Springer imprint is published by the registered company Springer Nature Switzerland AG
The registered company address is: Gewerbestrasse 11, 6330 Cham, Switzerland

Preface

Services account for a major part of the IT industry today. Companies increasingly like to focus on their core expertise area and use IT services to address all their peripheral needs. Services computing is a new science that aims to study and better understand the foundations of this highly popular industry. It covers the science and technology of leveraging computing and information technology to model, create, operate, and manage business services. The 2019 International Conference on Services Computing (SCC 2019) contributed to building the pillars of this important science and shaping the future of services computing.

SCC 2019 was part of the Services Conference Federation (SCF). SCF 2019 had the following ten collocated service-oriented sister conferences: 2019 International conference on Web Services (ICWS 2019), 2019 International Conference on Cloud Computing (CLOUD 2019), 2019 International Conference on Services Computing (SCC 2019), 2019 International Congress on Big Data (BigData 2019), 2019 International Conference on AI & Mobile Services (AIMS 2019), 2019 World Congress on Services (SERVICES 2019), 2019 International Congress on Internet of Things (ICIOT 2019), 2019 International Conference on Cognitive Computing (ICCC 2019), 2019 International Conference on Edge Computing (EDGE 2019), and 2019 International Conference on Blockchain (ICBC 2019). As the founding member of SCF, the First International Conference on Web Services (ICWS) was held in June 2003 in Las Vegas, USA. The First International Conference on Web Services—Europe 2003 (ICWS-Europe 2003) was held in Germany in October 2003. ICWS-Europe 2003 was an extended event of the 2003 International Conference on Web Services (ICWS 2003) in Europe. In 2004, ICWS-Europe was changed to the European Conference on Web Services (ECOWS), which was held in Erfurt, Germany. To celebrate its 16th birthday, SCF 2018 was held successfully in Seattle, USA.

SCC has been a prime international forum for researchers and industry practitioners alike to exchange the latest fundamental advances in the state of the art and practice of business modeling, business consulting, solution creation, service delivery, and software architecture design, development, and deployment.

This volume presents the accepted papers for SCC 2019, held in San Diego, USA, during June 25–30, 2019. For SCC 2019, we accepted nine full papers, including five research track papers and four application and industry track papers. Each was reviewed and selected by at least three independent members of the SCC 2019 international Program Committee. We are pleased to thank the authors, whose submissions and participation made this conference possible. We also want to express our thanks to the Organizing Committee and Program Committee members, for their dedication in helping to organize the conference and in reviewing the submissions. We would like to thank Prof. Dimitrios Georgakopoulos, who provided continuous support for this conference. We look forward to your great contributions as a volunteer, author, and conference participant for the fast-growing worldwide services innovations community.

May 2019

Joao Eduardo Ferreira
Aibek Musaev
Liang-Jie Zhang

Organization

General Chair

Dimitrios Georgakopoulos   Swinburne University of Technology, Australia

Program Chairs

Joao Eduardo Ferreira   Instituto de Matemática e Estatística, Brazil
Aibek Musaev   The University of Alabama, USA

Services Conference Federation (SCF 2019)

SCF 2019 General Chairs

Calton Pu   Georgia Tech, USA
Wu Chou   Essenlix Corporation, USA
Ali Arsanjani   8x8 Cloud Communications, USA

SCF 2019 Program Chair

Liang-Jie Zhang   Kingdee International Software Group Co., Ltd., China

SCF 2019 Finance Chair

Min Luo   Services Society, USA

SCF 2019 Industry Exhibit and International Affairs Chair

Zhixiong Chen   Mercy College, USA

SCF 2019 Operations Committee

Huan Chen   Kingdee International Software Group Co., Ltd., China
Liping Deng   Kingdee International Software Group Co., Ltd., China
Yishuang Ning   Tsinghua University, China
Sheng He   Tsinghua University, China

SCF 2019 Steering Committee

Calton Pu (Co-chair)   Georgia Tech, USA
Liang-Jie Zhang (Co-chair)   Kingdee International Software Group Co., Ltd., China

SCC 2019 Program Committee

Travis Atkison	The University of Alabama, USA
Karim Benouaret	Université Lyon 1, France
Sanjay Chaudhary	Ahmedabad University, India
Lizhen Cui	Shandong University, China
Yong-Yi Fanjiang	Fu Jen Catholic University
Kenneth Fletcher	University of Massachusetts Boston, USA
Pedro Furtado	University Coimbra/CISUC, Portugal
Kurt Geihs	University of Kassel, Germany
Alfredo Goldman	USP, Brazil
Zhe Jiang	The University of Alabama, USA
Shijun Liu	Shandong University, China
XiaoDong Liu	Institute of Computing Technology Chinese Academy of Sciences, China
Markus Lumpe	Swinburne University of Technology, Australia
Xin Luo	Chongqing University, China
Shang-Pin Ma	National Taiwan Ocean University
Massimo Mecella	Sapienza University of Rome, Italy
Seog Chan Oh	GM Research, USA
Marcio Katsumi Oikawa	Federal University of ABC, Brazil
Andre Luis Schwerz	Federal University of Technology Paraná (UTFPR), Brazil
Jun Shen	University of Wollongong, Australia
Kunal Suri	French Alternative Energies and Atomic Energy Commission (CEA), France
Yang Syu	Academia Sinica
Liang Tang	Google, USA
Dingwen Tao	The University of Alabama, USA
Quanwang Wu	Chongqing University, China
Yunni Xia	Chongqing University, China
Yu-Bin Yang	Nanjing University, China
Iling Yen	University of Texas at Dallas, USA
Muhammad Younas	Oxford Brookes University, UK
Jiantao Zhou	Inner Mongolia University, China
Shigeru Hosono	Tokyo University of Technology, Japan
Eleanna Kafeza	Athens University of Economics and Business, Greece

Contents

A Quality-Aware Web API Recommender System for Mashup Development

Kenneth K. Fletcher$^{(\boxtimes)}$ (iD)

University of Massachusetts Boston, Boston, MA 02125, USA
`kenneth.fletcher@umb.edu`

Abstract. The rapid increase in the number and diversity of web APIs with similar functionality, makes it challenging to find suitable ones for mashup development. In order to reduce the number of similarly functional web APIs, recommender systems are used. Various web API recommendation methods exist which attempt to improve recommendation accuracy, by mainly using some discovered relationships between web APIs and mashups. Such methods are basically incapable of recommending quality web APIs because they fail to incorporate web API quality in their recommender systems. In this work, we propose a method that considers the quality features of web APIs, to make quality web API recommendations. Our proposed method uses web API quality to estimate their relevance for recommendation. Specifically, we propose a matrix factorization method, with quality feature regularization, to make quality web API recommendations and also enhance recommendation diversity. We demonstrate the effectiveness of our method by conducting experiments on a real-world dataset from *www.programmableweb.com*. Our results not only show quality web API recommendations, but also, improved recommendation accuracy. In addition, our proposed method improves recommendation diversity by mitigating the negative Matthew effect of accumulated advantage, intrinsic to most existing web API recommender systems. We also compare our method with some baseline recommendation methods for validation.

Keywords: Mashup · Web API · Web API recommendation · Quality-Aware Recommendation · Matrix factorization · Mashup development

1 Introduction

Mashups represent a type of lightweight web applications, that compose existing web services/APIs in an agile manner [1]. Mashup technology helps shorten development periods and enhance the scalability of web applications [2]. Due to these advantages, several online mashup and web API repositories, such as *www.programmableweb.com*, have been established. In these repositories, there are large number of published web APIs, which mashup developers can compose, to create mashup solutions, for completing some customer's needs. For

© Springer Nature Switzerland AG 2019
J. E. Ferreira et al. (Eds.): SCC 2019, LNCS 11515, pp. 1–15, 2019.
https://doi.org/10.1007/978-3-030-23554-3_1

example, *www.programmableweb.com* has 19,669 web APIs, belonging to more than 400 predefined categories, as at October 2018 [3]. With such large number of web APIs, mashup developers are typically faced with the challenge of selecting suitable web APIs for mashup development. For this reason, recommendation techniques have become very important and popular because they reduce the amount of web APIs by presenting mashup developers with relevant web APIs to choose from.

The application of most traditional service recommender systems to web API recommendation is limited, because they lack some quality of service information and formal semantic specification, specific to web API recommendation [2]. However, there some few existing works that have proposed recommendation methods peculiar to web API recommendations. These methods are based on: (1) content similarity and topic modeling [4–8], (2) finding some relationship between mashups and web API invocation [2,5,6] or (3) exploiting various features such as web API description, tags, popularity and usage history to improve recommendation accuracy [4,6,9–12]. These works mostly skew the selection of web APIs towards popularity, which ultimately increases the Matthew effect of accumulated advantage [13]. This issue may sometimes cause mashup developers to miss out on potentially good and quality web APIs that are not popular [1]. An attempt to address this issue was proposed by Cao et al. [5]. Yet their proposed method, an integrated content and network-based web API recommendation method for mashup development, have a couple limitations: (1) the method focused so much on making unpopular web APIs popular with no consideration of the quality of these unpopular web APIs; and (2) their method employed memory-based collaborative filtering, with pearson correlation coefficient (PCC) as their similarity function. PCC, however, has been known to perform poorly in cases where the invocation relationship matrix between mashups and their invoked web APIs is very sparse [12].

In this work, we propose a method to address the above limitations, to provide relevant, quality, accurate and diverse web API recommendations for mashup development. Our method employs the quality model by Fletcher [1], developed specifically to analyze the quality of web APIs. The quality model uses a black-box approach to compute the quality of web APIs because web APIs have their internal details and complexity usually hidden. Our proposed method subsequently regularizes matrix factorization with web API quality features in order to provide quality web API recommendations. In addition, by incorporating the quality features into matrix factorization, our proposed method ensures improved recommendation accuracy and diversity, thereby mitigating the Matthew effect of accumulated advantage. The contributions of this work are summarized as follows:

1. We investigate and employ the black-box quality model proposed by Fletcher [1], to analyze the quality of web APIs, in order to make quality web API recommendations. By so doing, our proposed method considers the quality of web APIs during recommendation.

2. We propose a recommendation method that combines matrix factorization and the quality features, that describes the quality of web APIs, for web API recommendations. By incorporating the quality features into matrix factorization, our proposed method ensures improved recommendation accuracy and diversity, besides recommending quality web APIs.
3. We conduct experiments using real web API dataset, API-Dataset[1] [1], from *www.programmableweb.com*. This is to evaluate and validate our proposed method.

The rest of this paper is organized as follows: In Sect. 2, we discuss some results of an empirical study we performed as a motivation to our proposed method. In addition, we give some background information on matrix factorization. We present our proposed method in detail in Sect. 3, followed by our experiments, evaluations and results analysis in Sect. 4. In Sect. 5, we discuss some of the current state-of-the-art web API/service recommendation works. Finally, we conclude our paper and discuss some directions for our future work in Sect. 6.

2 Background

This section gives some background information relating to our proposed method. We first study the relationship between the quality of the different web APIs in our dataset and popularity (invocation frequency). Next, we present the quality model employed in our proposed method. Finally, we give a brief description of matrix factorization and the reason for our choice.

2.1 Empirical Study

Our empirical study focuses on studying one of the popular online web APIs and mashup repository, *www.programmableweb.com*. This is by far the largest online web API repository that contains over 19,000 web APIs, with various functionalities [3,7]. We use the API-Dataset [1], which was crawled from *www.programmableweb.com* in March 2018. The API-Dataset contains 12,879 web API records with 383 categories. Table 1 shows a list of the top 10 categories in our dataset. Each web API in our dataset is described by 19 fields such as name, description, authentication model, request and response formats, etc.

Research has shown that there is an imbalance in the frequency of different web API invocations in existing mashups [2]. Our study revealed that less than 7% of web APIs in our dataset have been invoked in existing mashups, while in contrast, about 93% of web APIs have not been invoked at all. The web API invocation imbalance is as a result of the negative Matthew effect of accumulated advantage; where popular web APIs are invoked frequently while unpopular ones are rarely invoked or not invoked at all. For instance, *Google Maps* web API, one of the most popular web APIs in our dataset, has been invoked 2,574 times,

---

[1] https://github.com/kkfletch/API-Dataset.

Table 1. Top 10 Web API Categories from *programmableweb.com* as at March 2018

Category	Number of Web APIs
Tools	787
Financial	583
Enterprise	486
eCommerce	434
Social	402
Messaging	388
Payments	374
Government	306
Mapping	295
Science	287

accounting for almost 17% of the total web API invocations in our dataset. Results from our study, however, showed that popularity of a web API does not necessarily indicate better web API, with respect to quality.

We selected all web APIs belonging to the *Mapping* category and compared each of them based on number of invocations and quality. We chose the *Mapping* category because it was one of the popular categories. Using the quality model proposed by Fletcher [1] (we discuss this model in detail in Sect. 2.2), we computed the quality of each web API in our dataset. Figure 1 shows a graph that compares the number of invocations and quality of web APIs (top 30 based on quality), belonging to the *Mapping* web API category. On the graph, the primary

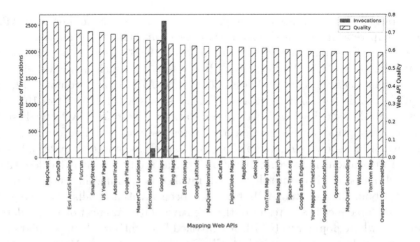

Fig. 1. Top 30 out of 295 Web APIs, based on Quality, belonging to the *Mapping* category from *www.programmableweb.com*.

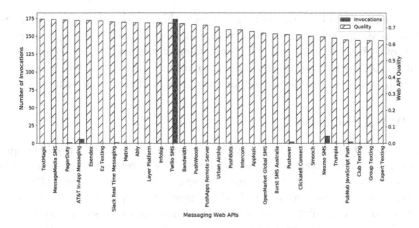

Fig. 2. Top 30 out of 388 Web APIs, based on Quality, belonging to the *Messaging* category from *www.programmableweb.com.*

y-axis indicates the number of invocations while the secondary y-axis is the web API quality. From the graph, it can be seen that *Google Maps* web API is the most popular, with respect to the number of invocations (i.e. 2,574 invocations). Yet there are several web APIs, also in the *Mapping* web API category, with better quality than *Google Maps* web API. In addition, we see from the graph that there are some web APIs like *CartoDB*, with very low number of invocation but has better quality.

To show such cases exist in other web API categories, we similarly analyzed the web APIs in the *Messaging* category. Figure 2 compares the top 30 web APIs, based on quality, against the number of invocations and quality of web APIs belonging to the *Messaging* category. From the figure, we see that there are several web APIs like *TextMagic*, *Ez Texting*, etc, that are of high quality, yet have not been invoked at all. There are however some popular web APIs with good quality. For instance, *Twilio SMS* web API, is the most popular web API in the *Messaging* category that also has good web API quality. However, our study reveals more and more web APIs, with very good quality, are not being invoked at all.

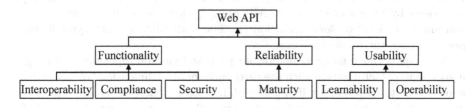

Fig. 3. Web API quality model based on Fletcher [1]

Therefore, there is the need to popularize these unpopular but quality web APIs for mashup development. One way to achieve this is by incorporating the quality of web APIs into web API recommender systems. In so doing, recommender systems will not only recommend quality web APIs, but will also provide enough diversity to include unpopular web APIs in their recommendations.

2.2 Web API Quality

To determine the quality of a service, we can analyze values from its quality of service (QoS) parameters, such as availability, reliability, response time, etc. These QoS values, however, are not easy to obtain with web APIs. This is because, web APIs typically hide their internal complexity and details and therefore external quality factors drive the evaluation of its suitability for integration into a mashup application [1,14]. For this reason, we adopt the quality model proposed by Fletcher [1], to define our black-box quality model for web APIs.

Figure 3 gives an overview of the quality features of a web API, which we organize along three main web API dimensions, namely *Functionality*, *Reliability* and *Usability*. The functionality of a web API can be refined by considering its *interoperability*, *compliance*, and *security* level [1]. Interoperability of a web API depends on its capability to be used in different and heterogeneous environments. Compliance is the ability of the web API to at least support one of the standard data formats. This in turn increases the interoperability level. The security of a web API is related to the protection mechanism that is used to rule access to the offered functionalities. Two main aspects are considered: SSL support and authentication mechanisms.

Reliability of a web API is measured with respect to its maturity. This is because the black-box approach does not allow one to evaluate the level of performance of a component under stated conditions for a stated period of time [1]. Reliability can be evaluated in terms of maturity, by considering the available statistics of usage of the component together with the frequency of its changes and updates.

The final dimension of a web API quality is usability. A web API's usability is evaluated in terms of understandability. Given the black-box approach, understandability can be evaluated by considering the web API documentation. Particularly relevant in the mashup scenario is the support offered to mashup composers by means of examples, API groups, blogs, or sample source codes, and any other kind of documentation [1]. The availability of each type of support increases the quality feature.

We employ this quality model for our proposed method. Specifically, we regularize matrix factorization with the three main quality dimensions of web APIs, namely: functionality, reliability, and usability. In so doing, we include the quality of web APIs into our proposed recommender system for quality web API recommendations.

2.3   Matrix Factorization

Matrix factorization is one of the widely used model-based collaborative filtering methods in recommender systems [15]. Although memory-based collaborative filtering methods are simple and intuitive, our choice of employing matrix factorization is due to its ability to successfully discover the underlying latent features in the interactions between users and items. In addition, it has exceptional scalability and predictive accuracy. Given that historical data are often placed in a two-dimensional matrix; user dimension and item dimension, matrix factorization characterizes both users and items by vectors of factors inferred from the interaction patterns between users and items, implied by the item-user matrix [2]. Basically, given a sparse user-API matrix $M^{m \times n}$, matrix factorization decomposes M into a product of two lower dimensionality rectangular matrices, $S^{m \times k}$ and $A^{n \times k}$ (i.e. $M = S \times A^T$), where:

 - k is the number of dimensions and $k < min(m, n)$,
 - S is the latent factor matrix of users, and
 - A is the latent factor matrix of web APIs.

S and A share the same latent space to characterize the two entities. The recommendation can then be performed by inferring and ranking the missing values of entries based on the lower dimensionality matrices, derived from the values of observable entries.

3   Quality-Aware Web API Recommender System

This section first gives an overview of the proposed method and thereafter describes the main modules that drives our method. Figure 4 shows the overview of the proposed method.

The functional profile information of assets (web APIs and mashups) are placed into a repository. We employ this dataset to construct the mashup-web API relation matrix from the historical invocation and user interactions. Here, we consider mashups as "users" and web APIs as "items", analogous to the typical user-item matrix. From this relations matrix, we retain only the invoked web APIs, as users' implicit preferences. We subsequently regularize matrix factorization by using the three quality dimensions and relation matrix.

When a mashup developer submits their textual mashup requirement, we identify the functionally similar web APIs using topic modeling techniques. We employ Hierarchical Dirichlet Process (HDP) [16] and Jensen-Shannon divergence [17] to obtain a list of web APIs matching the mashup developer's requirements. We subsequently, use this to filter the list of web APIs to be recommended. This is handled by the *Requirement-Web API Similarity* component in Fig. 4. We do not discuss the details of this component because it is not the focus in this work.

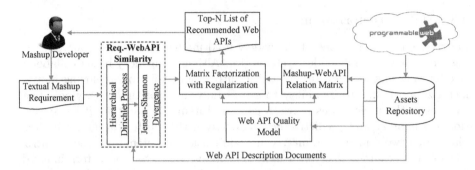

Fig. 4. Overview of the proposed regularized matrix factorization method with quality features for web API recommendation

3.1   Problem Definition

Let $U = \{u_1, u_2, u_3, ..., u_m\}$ be a set of users and $W = \{w_1, w_2, w_3, ..., w_n\}$ be a set of web APIs. We create an invocation matrix, $\mathbf{C} \in \mathbb{C}^{m \times n}$ between each user and web API, such that:

$$C_{u,w} \to I_{u \times w} \mid u \in U, w \in W \tag{1}$$

where I denotes the invocation and

$$c_{uw} = \begin{cases} 0 \text{ if } I = none \\ 1 \text{ if } otherwise \end{cases}$$

We use matrix factorization to map users and web APIs into two lower dimension spaces as described in Sect. 2.3. Let $S^T = (\alpha_1, \alpha_2, ..., \alpha_m)$, where α_u is the latent factor vector of user $\mathbf{u}$. Also, let $A^T = (\beta_1, \beta_2, ..., \beta_n)$, where β_w is the latent factor vector for web API $\mathbf{w}$. We can estimate the probability of a user u interacting with web API w as:

$$\hat{c}_{uw} = {\alpha_\mathbf{u}}^T \beta_\mathbf{w} \tag{2}$$

We can subsequently learn both latent factor vectors α_u and β_w by minimizing the $\mathcal{L}_2$ loss as:

$$L = \min_{S,A} \frac{1}{2} \sum_{u,w} h_{uw}(c_{uw} - \hat{c}_{uw})^2 + \frac{1}{2}\left(\lambda_\alpha \sum_{u=1}^{m} \parallel \alpha_u \parallel^2 + \lambda_\beta \sum_{w=1}^{n} \parallel \beta_w \parallel^2\right) \tag{3}$$

where $h_{u,w}$ is the weight of the interaction between user u and web API w. This is a hyperparameter to compensate the interaction between user u and web API w and also balances the number of non-zero and zero values in a sparse user-web API matrix [15]. λ_α and λ_β are used to adjust the importance of the regularization terms $\sum_u \parallel \alpha_u \parallel^2$ and $\sum_w \parallel \beta_w \parallel^2$.

For each web API $w \in W$, there is a quality property $Q(w)$, that indicates the quality of the web API w given as:

$$Q(w) = \frac{1}{3}\left(Q_F(w) + Q_R(w) + Q_B(w)\right) \tag{4}$$

where Q_F, Q_R and Q_B are the quality properties for functionality (F), reliability (R), and usability (B) quality dimensions respectively, as described in Sect. 2.2. Their formalized descriptions are as follows:

$$Q_F = \frac{1}{3}[(1 + \frac{|lang|}{k} + \frac{|dformat|}{l}) + 3comp + \frac{3}{5}sec] \tag{5}$$

where $lang$ and $dformat$ are the languages and data formats supported by the web API, and $comp$ and sec are compliance and security levels of the web API respectively.

$$Q_R = max\left(1 - \frac{cdate - ludate}{\frac{cdate - crdate}{|ver|}}, 0\right) \tag{6}$$

where $cdate$, $ludate$, and $crdate$ are the current date, last use date and creation date of the web API respectively, and ver is the set of version available for that web API.

$$Q_B = \begin{cases} 0 \text{ if } B \leq 0 \\ 1 \text{ if } B \geq \gamma \\ \frac{B}{\gamma} \text{ if } otherwise \end{cases} \tag{7}$$

where γ is the threshold of acceptable documentation for the usability quality dimension to be satisfied.

For each user $u \in U$, we utilize their historical web API invocations (n) and their associated quality properties to create the user's quality score, QS_u, defined as:

$$QS_u = \frac{1}{n}\sum_{i=1}^{n} Q(w_i) \tag{8}$$

Given a web API w, its quality property Q_w, and a user u's quality score QS_u, the satisfaction [18] of w, with respect to QS_u, is given as:

$$Sat_{QS_u}(w) = \begin{cases} 0 \text{ if } Q(w) \leq 0 \\ 1 \text{ if } Q(w) \geq QS_u \\ \frac{Q(w)}{QS_u} \text{ if } otherwise \end{cases} \tag{9}$$

3.2   Web API Recommendation Based on Quality

The ability of matrix factorization to easily include side information, such as our web API quality dimensions, is one of its greatest advantage [2]. Hence, once the user quality preferences are complete, we incorporate it into matrix factorization. Specifically, we combine those quality dimensions with matrix factorization (Eq. 3) to regularize the latent features of user quality on web APIs. Our regularized matrix factorization is as follows:

$$L = \min_{S,A} \frac{1}{2}\sum_{u,w} h_{uw}(c_{uw} - \hat{c}_{uw})^2 + \frac{1}{2}\sum_{D_{uv}\neq 0} \hat{h}_{uv}(D_{uv} - \alpha_u^T\theta_v - f_u - g_v)^2 +$$
$$\frac{1}{2}\lambda\left(\sum_u \parallel \alpha_u \parallel^2 + \sum_w \parallel \beta_w \parallel^2 + \sum_v \parallel \theta_v \parallel^2\right) \tag{10}$$

where:

- D be a shifted positive pointwise mutual information (SPPMI) [15] matrix constructed by user-web API quality patterns,
- θ is a $k \times 1$ latent representation vector of a user, and
- f and g are quality bias and quality context bias respectively [15].

Using the output from Eq. 10, we can then make quality web API recommendations to a target mashup developer.

4   Experiments and Results

We conducted several experiments to evaluate our proposed method. These experiments were done to ascertain the performance of our proposed method on web API recommendations compared to other existing recommendation methods, on quality and diversity. We discuss our experimental setup and results in this section.

4.1   Experimental Setup

We evaluate our proposed method using web API and mashup dataset, API-Dataset. See Sect. 2.1 for details on the dataset. We follow a 70/10/20 proportions for splitting the original dataset into training/validation/test sets [15]. For each baseline, we randomly divided our dataset into five different sets of 70/10/20 proportions also representing training/validation/test respectively. In Sect. 4.4, we present the average results from these five sets. All models were trained on the same set of hyperparameters which were tuned with the validation set. We set our regularization term $\lambda = 0.001$ and $\gamma = 75$.

4.2   Evaluation Metrics

We selected the following metrics to evaluate our method against because they are well-known to evaluate ranking-based methods.

Normalized Discounted Cumulative Gain (NDCG): Top-N DCG measures the ranking quality by placing stronger emphasis on having relevant items in the top-N.

$$DCG_p = \sum_{i=1}^{p} \frac{2^{rel_i} - 1}{\log_2(i+1)} \tag{11}$$

where rel_i is the graded relevance of the result at position i and p is a particular rank position. We normalize each cumulative gain at each position, since our ranking engine performance cannot be consistently achieved by using only DCG.

$$NDCG = \frac{DCG}{IDCG} \tag{12}$$

In a perfect ranking algorithm, $DCG = IDCG$, producing a NDCG of 1.0.

Recall: Top-N recall measures the sensitivity of the recommender system. It captures the effectiveness of the model in terms of outputting relevant predictions. It is computed as:

$$Recall@N = \frac{tP}{tP + fN} \tag{13}$$

where tP and fN are true positive and false negative respectively. Higher recall values indicates better performance.

Mean Average Precision (MAP): MAP for a set of ranking results is the mean of the average precision scores for each ranking.

4.3 Baselines

We compare our model to the following baselines:

- **Matrix Factorization (MF):** this method uses weighted matrix factorization with $\mathcal{L}_2$-norm regularization [19].
- **Fuzzy Logic-based Method (FLM)** this is fuzzy-logic based approach for recommending items based on quality [20].
- **Personalized Collaborative Filtering (PCF):** this method uses Pearson Correlation Coefficient to compute the similarity between web APIs and a fuzzy set approach to find the similarity between user preferences to make recommendations [12].
- **Mashup Recommendation with API Co-Invocations (MRAC):** employs a probabilistic matrix factorization approach with implicit correlation regularization to improve recommendation accuracy and diversity [2].
- **Integrated Content and Network-based Service Clustering for Web API Recommendation (ICNSC):** this method uses an integrated content and network-based solution, which leverages the interrelationship among mashup services to extract latent topics to produce mashup clusters for web API recommendation [5].
- **Proposed model (PM):** this is the proposed model in this work.

4.4 Experimental Results

Figure 5 shows our performance results of our proposed method compared to the baseline models, based on Recall, NDCG, MAP and quality satisfaction of recommended web APIs. For each of the first three metrics, we varied the top-N values from 10–100 at intervals of 10. Figures 5a–c show the results for Recall, MAP and NDCG respectively. To compare the models based on quality satisfaction, we used the satisfaction functions described in Sect. 3.1 to find the satisfaction of recommended web APIs from the five different datasets. Figure 5d show the results for the quality satisfaction comparison.

Overall, using our dataset, our proposed model (PM) outperformed the other baselines. On an average, our model (PM) improved Recall by 34%, NDCG by

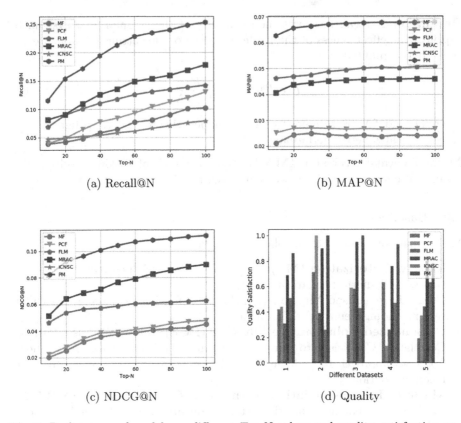

(a) Recall@N

(b) MAP@N

(c) NDCG@N

(d) Quality

Fig. 5. Performance of models on different Top-N values and quality satisfaction on the different 5 datasets.

23% and MAP by 26%. From Fig. 5d, we can observe that the quality of web API recommendations from our model is not only high but consistent, compared to other baseline methods that do not consider quality. These experimental results confirms the effectiveness of our proposed model.

ICNSC method performed worst than expected for all metrics. Our experiments revealed it is due to pearson correlation coefficient (PCC) similarity function that was employed. In the mashup application domain, since there are very less web APIs that are invoked, the invocation relationship matrix between mashup clusters and their invoked web APIs will be very sparse. PCC has however, been known to perform poorly in cases where the invocation relationship matrix between mashups and their invoked web APIs is very sparse [12]. MRAC performed next to our proposed method (PM), outperforming all other baseline methods on NDCG. This is because, the co-invocation method that MRAC method employs results in better diversity.

5   Related Work

Most existing web API recommendation methods focus on improving the accuracy and sometimes diversity of recommendations and rarely focus on quality. Yao et al. [2] proposed a probabilistic matrix factorization approach with implicit correlation regularization to improve the accuracy of API recommendations for mashup development. In the same light, Xia et al. [7] proposed a category-aware API clustering and distributed recommendation solution to enhance the accuracy of API recommendations. In addition, a method based on clustering and web API recommendation for mashup development was proposed by Cao et al. [5]. In this work, Cao et al. [5] proposed an integrated content and network-based solution which leverages the interrelationship among mashup services to extract latent topics to further produce mashup clusters. These works however, do not consider quality in their recommendation methods.

Similarly, in an attempt to improve accuracy and diversity in API recommendation, Gao et al. [21] adopts a learning technique which uses the geometric properties of data in high dimensions to implement clustering and dimensionality reduction (termed Manifold learning). The proposed algorithm first performs a functional similarity-based clustering and then utilizes manifold ranking algorithm to assign APIs to the generated mashup clusters. This approach like in most cases is popularity and functional-similarity oriented with no much attention to the quality of the APIs. Li et al. [22], also proposed a method for API recommendation, using a probabilistic model. In their work, they model the relationships among mashups, APIs and tags, via latent topic modeling. Their method however, is based on topic popularity and topic relevance, which was also the focus of Gao et al. [21]. These solutions do not also consider quality.

Xue et. al. [23] exploits the strength of deep learning models such as Convolutional Neural Networks (CNN), Long-Short Term Memory neural networks (LSTM) and other machine learning classifiers, together with Natural Language Processing (NLP), to produce an automatic generation and recommendation solution for API Mashups. Rahman et al. [6] also proposed a matrix factorization based solution which incorporates mashup service relationships to make web API recommendations. This proposed method by Rahman et. al. uses the Integrated Content and Network-Based service clustering technique proposed by Cao et al. [24].

Although most works discussed above are not quality oriented, most of them utilized the matrix factorization method for their recommendations. Similar to our work, Tejeda-Lorente et al. [20], proposed a method to recommend items based on quality. Their method uses a fuzzy linguistic approach from fuzzy sets theory. They used this concept to model qualitative information of items to infer their quality. Their work however has some limitations: (1) their method allows users to specify their quality preferences qualitatively using fuzzy linguistic terms. It is generally challenging to obtain accurate user preferences due to their dynamic nature. This makes their model impractical to web API recommendations. (2) their model does not provide a solid quality model to assess the quality of web APIs. Our proposed method, however, addresses these limitations.

6   Conclusion

In this work we have proposed a method, which considers web API quality to make quality web API recommendations, while improving recommendation accuracy and diversity. Our method regularizes matrix factorization using the three web API quality dimensions, namely, functionality, reliability and usability for quality web API recommendations. We have shown how our proposed method takes advantage of external quality factors of web APIs to drive the evaluation of its quality for integration into mashup applications. This we did, to provide quality web API recommendations and also to improve recommendation accuracy and diversity. Experiments performed shows that our proposed method outperforms other baseline methods. For our future work, we will run more experiments to ascertain the impact of some key parameters on our model. In addition, we will validate our model against more existing methods.

References

1. Fletcher, K.K.: A quality-based web API selection for mashup development using affinity propagation. In: Ferreira, J.E., Spanoudakis, G., Ma, Y., Zhang, L.-J. (eds.) SCC 2018. LNCS, vol. 10969, pp. 153–165. Springer, Cham (2018). https://doi.org/10.1007/978-3-319-94376-3_10

2. Yao, L., Wang, X., Sheng, Q.Z., Benatallah, B., Huang, C.: Mashup recommendation by regularizing matrix factorization with API co-invocations. IEEE Trans. Serv. Comput. (2018)

3. Santos, W.: Research shows interest in providing APIs still high. https://www.programmableweb.com/news/research-shows-interest-providing-apis-still-high/research/2018/02/23. Accessed 18 Oct 2018

4. Zhong, Y., Fan, Y., Tan, W., Zhang, J.: Web service recommendation with reconstructed profile from mashup descriptions. IEEE Trans. Autom. Sci. Eng. **15**(2), 468–478 (2018)

5. Cao, B., Liu, X., Rahman, M.M., Li, B., Liu, J., Tang, M.: Integrated content and network-based service clustering and web APIs recommendation for mashup development. IEEE Trans. Serv. Comput. (2017)

6. Rahman, M.M., Liu, X., Cao, B.: Web API recommendation for mashup development using matrix factorization on integrated content and network-based service clustering. In: IEEE International Conference on Services Computing (SCC), pp. 225–232. IEEE (2017)

7. Xia, B., Fan, Y., Tan, W., Huang, K., Zhang, J., Wu, C.: Category-aware API clustering and distributed recommendation for automatic mashup creation. IEEE Trans. Serv. Comput. **8**(5), 674–687 (2015)

8. Buqing, C., Tang, M., Huang, X.: CSCF: a mashup service recommendation approach based on content similarity and collaborative filtering. Int. J. Grid Distrib. Comput. **7**(2), 163–172 (2014)

9. Li, H., Liu, J., Cao, B., Tang, M., Liu, X., Li, B.: Integrating tag, topic, co-occurrence, and popularity to recommend web APIs for mashup creation. In: IEEE International Conference on Services Computing (SCC), pp. 84–91. IEEE (2017)

10. Fletcher, K.K.: A method for dealing with data sparsity and cold-start limitations in service recommendation using personalized preferences. In: IEEE International Conference on Cognitive Computing (ICCC), pp. 72–79, June 2017

11. Gu, Q., Cao, J., Peng, Q.: Service package recommendation for mashup creation via mashup textual description mining. In: IEEE International Conference on Web Services (ICWS), pp. 452–459, June 2016
12. Fletcher, K.K., Liu, X.F.: A collaborative filtering method for personalized preference-based service recommendation. In: IEEE International Conference on Web Services, pp. 400–407, June 2015
13. Rigney, D.: The Matthew Effect: How Advantage Begets Further Advantage. Columbia University Press, New York (2010)
14. Cappiello, C., Daniel, F., Matera, M.: A quality model for mashup components. In: Gaedke, M., Grossniklaus, M., Díaz, O. (eds.) ICWE 2009. LNCS, vol. 5648, pp. 236–250. Springer, Heidelberg (2009). https://doi.org/10.1007/978-3-642-02818-2_19
15. Tran, T., Lee, K., Liao, Y., Lee, D.: Regularizing matrix factorization with user and item embeddings for recommendation. In: Proceedings of the 27th ACM International Conference on Information and Knowledge Management, CIKM 2018, pp. 687–696. ACM, New York (2018)
16. Teh, Y.W., Jordan, M.I., Beal, M.J., Blei, D.M.: Hierarchical Dirichlet processes. J. Am. Stat. Assoc. **101**(476), 1566–1581 (2006)
17. Fuglede, B., Topsoe, F.: Jensen-Shannon divergence and Hilbert space embedding. In: Proceedings of International Symposium on Information Theory, ISIT 2004, June 2004
18. Fletcher, K.: A method for aggregating ranked services for personal preference based selection. Int. J. Web Serv. Res. (IJWSR) **16**(2), 1–23 (2019)
19. Hu, Y., Koren, Y., Volinsky, C.: Collaborative filtering for implicit feedback datasets. In: Eighth IEEE International Conference on Data Mining, pp. 263–272, December 2008
20. Tejeda-Lorente, Á., Porcel, C., Peis, E., Sanz, R., Herrera-Viedma, E.: A quality based recommender system to disseminate information in a university digital library. Inf. Sci. **261**, 52–69 (2014)
21. Gao, W., Chen, L., Wu, J., Gao, H.: Manifold-learning based API recommendation for mashup creation. In: IEEE International Conference on Web Services (ICWS), pp. 432–439. IEEE (2015)
22. Li, C., Zhang, R., Huai, J., Sun, H.: A novel approach for API recommendation in mashup development. In: IEEE International Conference on Web Services (ICWS), pp. 289–296. IEEE (2014)
23. Xue, Q., Liu, L., Chen, W., Chuah, M.C.: Automatic generation and recommendation for API mashups. In: 16th IEEE International Conference on Machine Learning and Applications (ICMLA), pp. 119–124. IEEE (2017)
24. Cao, B., et al.: Mashup service clustering based on an integration of service content and network via exploiting a two-level topic model. In: IEEE International Conference on Web Services (ICWS), pp. 212–219. IEEE (2016)

Practical Verification of Data Encryption for Cloud Storage Services

Jinxia Fang[1,2,3], Limin Liu[2,3(✉)], and Jingqiang Lin[2,3]

[1] School of Cyber Security,
University of Chinese Academy of Sciences, Beijing, China
[2] State Key Laboratory of Information Security, Institute of Information
Engineering, Chinese Academy of Sciences, Beijing, China
`liulimin@iie.ac.cn`
[3] Data Assurance and Communication Security Research Center,
Chinese Academy of Sciences, Beijing, China

Abstract. Sensitive data is usually encrypted to protect against data leakage and unauthorized access for cloud storage services. Generally, the remote user has no knowledge of the actual data format stored in the cloud, even though a cloud server promises to store the data with encryption. Although a few works utilize data encapsulation and remote data checking to detect whether the sensitive data is protected securely in the cloud, they still suffer from a number of limitations, such as heavy computational cost at the user side and poor practicality, that would hinder their adoptions. In this paper, we propose a practical verification scheme to allow users to remotely evaluate the actually deployed data encryption protection in the cloud. We employ the pseudo-random number generator and present a data encapsulation solution, which can benefit users with significant cost savings. By imposing monetary rewards or penalties, our proposed scheme can help ensure that the cloud server stores data encrypted at rest honestly. Extensive experiments are conducted to further demonstrate the efficiency and practicality of the proposed scheme.

Keywords: Cloud storage service · Data encapsulation ·
Encryption verification · Performance evaluation

1 Introduction

Cloud storage service has already become an indispensable part of the process in business. More and more users outsource their sensitive data (such as confidential e-mails, government documents, company financial data, etc.) to the cloud for enjoying the on-demand, convenient and excellent storage service. However, according to the survey [5] conducted by RedLock, more than half of organizations that use cloud storage services have experienced data breaches in the past year. In order to prevent data leakage and unauthorized access of sensitive data

© Springer Nature Switzerland AG 2019
J. E. Ferreira et al. (Eds.): SCC 2019, LNCS 11515, pp. 16–31, 2019.
https://doi.org/10.1007/978-3-030-23554-3_2

from cloud storage services, an effective approach is to keep data encrypted at rest using cryptography technique.

Client-side encryption and server-side encryption are two primary strategies to protect data at rest for the cloud server, such as Amazon S3 [2], Microsoft Azure [3], Alibaba Cloud [1]. The main difference between them is the management of the encryption key. More precisely, the secret key in server-side encryption is retained by the server whereas the key is only kept by the user in client-side one. Because the cloud server cannot obtain the key, client-side encryption is effective to prevent the cloud server from cheating and storing the plaintext at rest. Accordingly, we do not consider client-side encryption in this paper.

Although the specific implementation of data encryption and related security practices are severely restricted by the *Service Level Agreement* (SLA), one problem is lack of the necessary visibility for users to verify that these security measures are implemented correctly. The cloud server has an incentive to cheat due to various reasons, including deliberately being lazy to save computational cost and ignore data encryption, or being so negligent as to cause wrong operations. Unless data leakage and economic losses have occurred, users are mostly unaware of the actually deployed security measures in the cloud.

To verify that users' data is stored securely, van Dijk et al. [12] first proposed a verification framework of data encryption for cloud services. In this framework, a time-consuming data encapsulation process is introduced to increase the transformation time from plaintext to encapsulated data finally stored in the cloud. Based on resource requirements for the cloud, they designed three hourglass schemes which are used to implement data encapsulation, namely RSA-based, Permutation-based and the Butterfly scheme. However, in these three schemes, users have to do all encryption and data encapsulation operations. Meanwhile, these schemes bring considerable overhead in small and frequent data accesses and updates. Later, Hu et al. [15] considered data updates by introducing a well-designed lookup table, but it still did not solve the problem that users bear significant computational cost. In order to enhance users' experience and boost the practicality of verification, lower computational complexity at the user side could be considered in verification technique of data encryption for cloud storage services.

This paper proposes a secure and practical verification approach to ensure the confidentiality protection for cloud data. Our proposal extends the concept of [15] without losing any of the desirable properties. Specifically, the cloud server conducts all encryption and data encapsulation operations by introducing the pseudo-random number generator and the lookup table to randomize the process of encapsulation. Users in our scheme only implement a small amount of above operations, which makes it possible to bring significant cost savings to users. Besides, the hash function and AES are combined to construct verifiable tags, and then these tags are stored with the cloud server. By issuing a random challenge against several randomly selected data blocks, the user can repeatedly query the cloud server to ensure that the data is correctly and fully stored.

We have the following contributions in this paper:

- We first propose a practical verification scheme of data encryption to release users from significant computational overhead.
- Theoretical analysis shows that our proposed scheme is sufficient to ensure that the cloud server correctly stores data encrypted at rest.
- In practice, extensive experiments further demonstrate the practicality and efficiency of our proposal.

The rest of this paper is organized as follows. Section 2 reviews related works for cloud security. Section 3 introduces the system model, threat model and design goals. We describe the design of our proposed data encryption verification scheme in Sect. 4, and explore the security analysis of our proposal in Sect. 5. Then we evaluate the performance of the scheme in Sect. 6. Finally, we conclude this paper in Sect. 7.

2 Related Works

Abundant works have been proposed to meet verification requirements of different security properties provided in the SLA. Provable Data Possession (PDP) [9] allows a user to verify that his data is fully intact in the remote cloud. Concurrently, Juels et al. [17] proposed a more secure concept called Proofs of Retrievability (POR), which convinces a user that he can retrieve the target file without downloading this file. Both techniques have been advanced in many aspects over recent years, including supporting for data update [23,24,26], combining data deduplication with integrity auditing [6,8,16,19], and achieving shared data integrity auditing [13,21,22,27]. Recently, Armknecht et al. [7] explored the unified model, Mirror, to prove data replication and retrievability for cloud services. Gorke et al. [14] combined data retrievability and data recoverability to provide an assurance whether the data can be recovered or irreparably damaged. In [11], Bowers et al. proposed a theoretical data redundancy verification framework, called the Remote Assessment of Fault Tolerance (RAFT). The core idea of RAFT lies in that the data owner and the cloud server must reach an agreement on the file layout information ahead of schedule. Unfortunately, disclosing the file layout details is not supported by the cloud in general. Without publishing the file layout information, Wang et al. [25] built response time profiles for each file placement to evaluate the data redundancy for cloud services. Long et al. [20] designed a dynamic PDP scheme of multiple copies by exploiting the AVL tree. Besides, network latency measurement is utilized to check whether the cloud server replicates the data in various geo-locations [10,18].

The goal of our proposed scheme is the verification of confidentiality protection to prevent against data leakage for cloud storage services. The literature [15] reaches a similar goal by using the lookup table to transform the ciphertext to encapsulated file before outsourcing. The encapsulated file, not plaintext or ciphertext, is actually kept in the disk of the cloud. In order to timely respond to the challenges issued by the data user, the retention of encapsulated file is the only reasonable strategy for the cloud server. In fact, compared with the honest cloud server, the dishonest one who wishes to hold plaintext needs to cost extra storage and computational overheads to return the correct proof to the data user within a certain time threshold. However, users in [15] must conduct the whole complicated process of encryption and data encapsulation, which would hinder the adoption of this scheme. In this paper, we address this shortcoming and greatly lower the computational overhead at the user side, simultaneously preserve all the advantages of [15]. Our proposal mainly focuses on the solution to ease users from considerable computational complexity and enhance users' experience. That is the major difference between [15] and our scheme.

3   Problem Formulation

As expressed in Sect. 2, none of previous works till now have explored the solution to enable data users to verify that data is stored securely while releasing them from considerable computational cost. To meet this challenge of enhancing users' experience and boosting the practicality of verification solution, we propose an efficient and practical verification scheme of data encryption for cloud storage services. This section explains the system model, threat model and design goals.

3.1   System Model

The system model in this paper involves two different entities: data user and cloud server. The data user can be either a person or an enterpriser that has a large-scale sensitive data F, which will be outsourced to the remote cloud server. The cloud server would offer a centralized, shared and massive storage service to store private user data. There are several types of storage service, such as file, object and block-based service. In this paper, we focus mainly on block-based storage service. It is worthy to note that the proposed scheme also applies to other storage services.

The cloud server first encrypts F to obtain ciphertext G, and then performs data encapsulation operation to transform G to encapsulated file H, which is actually stored in the hard disk of cloud. In other words, F is finally stored in the encapsulated form H in the cloud. The user constructs verifiable tags, and outsources these tags to the cloud server. At a later time, the data user frequently issues a challenge to verify the storage of H by the cloud server, and receives the corresponding response as proof from the cloud server over a time period. Afterwards, the user checks the correctness of proof to judge whether the cloud server is honest to correctly and entirely store H.

The cloud server is assumed to have enormous and cheap computational power and I/O capability, which are far beyond that of the user. Therefore, a further requirement on the user side is to minimize users' cost in terms of computation and communication, to enhance users' experience and improve the practicality of verification.

3.2 Threat Model

For simplicity and realism, the cloud server is considered as "cheap-and-lazy" in our model, which is similar to related works on cloud security [11,25]. The server may store the plaintext F with either cheap or lazy behavior. Specifically, the "cheap" server is incapable of implementing necessary security measures, such as misoperations of internal staffs. The server who acts in a "lazy" fashion ignores data confidentiality protection to reduce its computational cost and management overhead.

In the context of our model, we do not consider malicious servers because it is technically infeasible to protect data confidentiality against malicious servers till date. A malicious server storing plaintext F may be viewed as expending arbitrarily large storage resources to store H for responding appropriately to users' challenges. However, it takes double storage consumption for the malicious server to cheat, which is not desired by the cheap-and-lazy server.

3.3 Design Goals

Under the aforementioned model, to enable practical and efficient verification of data encryption over cloud storage services for greatly reducing computational overhead at the user side, our design goals are summarized as follows.

- **Practicability:** To be more realistic, considering burdensome data encryption and encapsulation are conducted by the cloud server, our proposed scheme is designed to release resource-constrained users from significant computational cost.
- **Security:** Our scheme aims to meet the security requirement that the retention of H is the only reasonable strategy for the cloud server to respond to challenges issued by the user within a short period of time.
- **Efficiency:** The scheme is also designed to gain effective verification with low communication and computational overheads.

4 The Proposed Scheme

In this section, in order to overcome the shortcoming of the solution [15], we propose a practical and efficient verification scheme which is resilient against the cheap-and-lazy adversary. We first give the general framework of the proposed scheme, and then elaborate on the specific procedure.

4.1 Overview

Considering the approach of that the user may challenge the server on the ciphertext, under the assumption that it is usually fast for the server to apply symmetric encryption algorithms, the transformation from plaintext to ciphertext could be easily done on the fly. Therefore, it will allow the server to store data in plaintext without being detected.

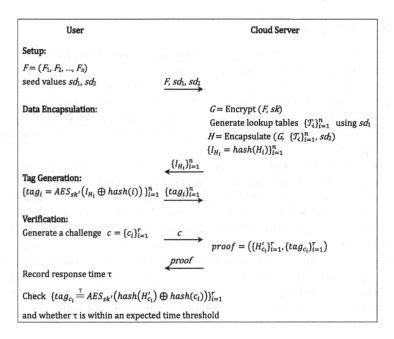

Fig. 1. The general framework of the proposed verification scheme of data encryption.

To meet this challenge, the ciphertext G would be transformed to encapsulated file H for data confidentiality protection. The proposed scheme aims to ensure that the cloud server stores H at rest correctly and fully, and simultaneously meets the design goals proposed in Sect. 3.3.

Figure 1 provides the framework of our proposal that mainly comprises the following four phases: *Setup*, *Data Encapsulation*, *Tag Generation* and *Verification*. In the *Setup* phase, the user uploads plaintext F, as well as some parameters for subsequent use, to the cloud server. During the *Data Encapsulation* phase, the cloud server performs the transformation from F to G then to H, generates hash value for each block of H and sends all the values to the user. The user constructs verifiable tags in the *Tag Generation* phase, by using hash values which are returned from the server. The last phase, *Verification*, is achieved to assure the user that the cloud server has retained the intact H by aperiodically issuing a challenge. The first three phases are executed only once, whereas the last one is repeatedly executed until data is erased from the cloud. Next, we present the detailed construction of our proposal.

4.2 Setup

Initially, let F denote n equally-sized data blocks, i.e., $F = (F_1, F_2, ..., F_n)$. The data user creates two seed values sd_1 and sd_2. Note that sd_1 is used for generating a number of lookup tables and decapsulating data, and sd_2 is used for data encapsulation. Later, the user uploads F, sd_1 and sd_2 together to the remote cloud.

4.3   Data Encapsulation

With the shared secret key sk by the cloud server and user, the cloud server adopts traditional encryption algorithms such as AES to encrypt plaintext F to ciphertext $G = (G_1, G_2, ..., G_n)$. Specifically, the cloud server first divides each block F_i into m data items, each of which has l bits (typically $l = 256$). Then each item in F is encrypted to corresponding item in G using a certain encryption algorithm and sk. Finally, all the encrypted items are concatenated into the ciphertext G.

The server generates n distinct random values as a set of salts $\{s_1, s_2, ..., s_n\}$ by utilizing the pseudo-random number generator, which takes sd_1 as input. Each random value is represented as a bit string of length l_n. For each block G_i, the server first invokes Algorithm 1 (The symbol "$||$" means concatenation.) to build a corresponding lookup table T_i with salt s_i, which is introduced in [15]. As described in Algorithm 1, parameters l_k and l_v ($l_k < l_v$) can be adjusted to increase the flexibility with multiple values. The table T_i contains an array L_i of 2^{l_k} elements and 2^{l_k} linked lists, which are numbered from 0 to $2^{l_k} - 1$ respectively. L_i records the specific length of each linked list in T_i. It be note worthy that lookup tables are built differently with different salts.

Algorithm 1. The algorithm for the generation of the lookup table T_i

---

Input: parameters l_k and l_v, salt s_i
Output: lookup table T_i

1: Construct an empty lookup table T_i;
2: **for** each $str \in \{0, 1\}^{l_v}$ **do**
3:     $u = hash(s_i || str) \bmod 2^{l_k}$;
4:     Insert str into the u-th linked list in T_i;
5:     $L_i[u] = L_i[u] + 1$;
6: **return** T_i

Based on multiple lookup tables $\{T_1, T_2, ..., T_n\}$, the server invokes Algorithm 2 to transform the ciphertext G to encapsulated file H. First, each block G_i is divided into w pieces, each of which is a l_k-bit binary string.[1] Second, with the lookup table T_i, each piece $G_{i,j}$, $j = 1, 2, ..., w$, is transformed to $H_{i,j}$. During the transformation process, by using the pseudo-random number generator which takes sd_2 as input, the server generates a random value a_u to compute $v = a_u \bmod L_i[G_{i,j}]$, where $L_i[G_{i,j}]$ is the length of the $G_{i,j}$-th linked list in T_i.[2] Then, the v-th element in the $G_{i,j}$-th linked list of T_i is picked as $H_{i,j}$. All the transformed pieces are concatenated into H. Finally, the file H, not plaintext F or ciphertext G, is ultimately stored in the cloud.

---

[1] Suppose that the size of G_i is a multiple of l_k. If not, we may add some padding to the last piece.
[2] Because $G_{i,j}$ has l_k bits, $0 \le G_{i,j} \le 2^{l_k} - 1$.

Next, the server calculates all the hash values of blocks of H to form $I_H = (I_{H_1}, I_{H_2}, ..., I_{H_n})$, where $I_{H_i} = hash(H_i)$ for $i = 1, 2, ..., n$ and $hash()$ is a hash function such as MD5. Afterwards, I_H is sent back to the user.

Algorithm 2. The algorithm for the encapsulation of the ciphertext G

Input: the ciphertext $G = (G_1, G_2, ..., G_n)$, lookup tables $\{T_1, T_2, ..., T_n\}$, sd_2 and l_k
Output: $H = (H_1, H_2, ..., H_n)$

1: Generate a series of random numbers $\{a_1, a_2, ...\}$, using sd_2 as a seed of pseudo-random number generator;
2: $u = 1$;
3: **for** each $i \in [1, n]$ **do**
4:     Divide G_i into w pieces, $G_i = (G_{i,1}, G_{i,2}, ..., G_{i,w})$, each of which is l_k bits;
5:     **for** each $j \in [1, w]$ **do**
6:         $v = a_u \bmod L_i[G_{i,j}]$;
7:         $H_{i,j} = T_i[G_{i,j}][v]$;
8:         $u = u + 1$;
9:     Concatenate these transformed pieces to form $H_i = (H_{i,1}, H_{i,2}, ..., H_{i,w})$;
10: **return** $H = (H_1, H_2, ..., H_n)$

At the end of this phase, the data user is assured that the collection I_H of hash values is correct for plaintext F with high probability. More specifically, the user implements data encapsulation operation on the t randomly queried blocks, where $0 \leq t \leq n$. As long as t hash values generated by the user are equal to the corresponding hash values in I_H returned from the server, the user would be convinced that I_H is correct and the server conducts the process of data encapsulation properly.

In our proposed scheme, the user can accomplish an expected confidence probability by adjusting the number t of queried blocks, which can be treated as a tunable parameter.

4.4   Tag Generation

With all the hash values I_H, the data user generates the verifiable tag for each block of H following the equation below:

$$tag_i = AES_{sk'}(I_{H_i} \oplus hash(i)), \tag{1}$$

where the secret key sk' is only owned by the user. Then, these tags are uploaded to and stored at the server.

4.5   Verification

To detect possible misbehavior by the cloud server, the user can check if the server still stores H at rest by issuing a random challenge $c = (c_1, c_2, ..., c_r)$.

The challenge c indicates r specific blocks of H which the user wants to detect. Here, $1 \leq r \leq n$, and $1 \leq c_i \leq n$ for $i = 1, 2, ..., r$. With the challenge c, the cloud server retrieves and returns corresponding encapsulated blocks, as well as corresponding tags uploaded by the user. Thus, the proof determined by c consists of two parts: $\{H'_{c_i}\}_{i=1}^r$ and $\{tag_{c_i}\}_{i=1}^r$.

Once the proof is received by the user within a certain period of time, the tag of each challenged block is recalculated as

$$tag'_{c_i} = AES_{sk'}(hash(H'_{c_i}) \oplus hash(c_i)). \tag{2}$$

Crucially, if the response time is within an expected time threshold, and meanwhile tag_{c_i} is equal to tag'_{c_i} for each item c_i in c, the data user outputs "true" which means that the cloud server is honest. Otherwise, "false" should be the output to show that the cloud server is dishonest.

For each verification, when setting the expected time threshold, the user should consider the number of queried blocks, each block size and network latency.

4.6 Data Access and Updating

Data Access. Suppose that a user wants to access one block in plaintext, decapsulating this block of H could be easily operated as specified in Algorithm 3. Specifically, the first step is to obtain the corresponding ciphertext block using hash and modular operations, and the second step is to generate the plaintext block using the decryption algorithm with the shared secret key sk.

Algorithm 3. The algorithm for the decapsulation of block H_i

---

Input: H_i, s_i, sk, l_k and l_v
Output: F_i
1: Divide H_i into w pieces, $H_i = (H_{i,1}, H_{i,2}, ..., H_{i,w})$, each of which is l_v bits;
2: **for** each $j \in [1, w]$ **do**
3:     $G_{i,j} = hash(s_i||H_{i,j}) \bmod 2^{l_k}$;
4: Concatenate these pieces to form $G_i = (G_{i,1}, G_{i,2}, ..., G_{i,w})$;
5: $F_i = Decrypt(G_i, sk)$;
6: **return** F_i

Data Updating. When the user needs to update some blocks, the cloud server should perform some computations, including encryption, corresponding lookup table generation and encapsulation again. The server recomputes hash value for each updated encapsulated blocks, and returns these hash values to the user.

By recalculating part of these hash values locally and comparing them with corresponding hash values which are received from the server, the user can verify (with overwhelming probability) that data updating is handled correctly. Later, new tags for updated blocks are recalculated according to the Eq. (1), and uploaded to replace old tags in the cloud.

5   Security Analysis

Considering a misbehaved cloud server who wishes to store plaintext F at rest for cheating and saving computational resource by falsely claiming to protect data confidentiality. In order to respond to challenges frequently issued by the user, the cloud server needs to cost extra storage to store the following information: the verifiable tags for H, sd_1 used in lookup table generation and data decapsulation, sd_2 and n lookup tables for data encapsulation. Thus, the storage overhead of a misbehaved cloud server for cheating is probably expressed as $|F| + \sum_{i=1}^{n} |T_i| - |H|$, where $|H| = \frac{l_v}{l_k}|F|$. Since the storage cost of one lookup table is about $(l_k + l_v) \cdot 2^{l_k} + l_v \cdot 2^{l_v}$ bits. Accordingly, as long as the size of each plaintext block F_i is not more than $\frac{l_k}{l_v - l_k} \cdot ((l_k + l_v) \cdot 2^{l_k} + l_v \cdot 2^{l_v})$ bits, there is no economic incentive for the cloud server to be misbehaved, such as save storage cost. As we can see that the maximum size of F_i mainly relies on l_k and l_v. Some cases are depicted in Table 1.

Table 1. Maximum size of each plaintext block

l_k, l_v	16, 20	18, 22	20, 24	22, 26	24, 28
Maximum size (MB)	11	55.125	267.5	1276	6000

Note that the misbehaved cloud server may not store these lookup tables to reduce storage overhead. In this case, in order to construct correct proofs, the cloud server must frequently perform too time-consuming generation of corresponding lookup tables to respond to the user in time. Moreover, it still brings considerable computational and storage overheads to the faulty cloud server.

According to the analysis above, our proposed scheme forces a misbehaved cloud server to recalculate queried blocks of H on the fly in an expensively slow and detectable fashion. In other words, our scheme creates a monetary incentive for the cloud server to store H correctly and fully.

6   Performance Evaluation

In this section, we conduct a thorough experimental evaluation of the proposed scheme on a local machine, which is a Linux operation system with Intel Core i5 3.30 GHz. All components are written in C++ language. We use the OpenSSL library [4] for all the hash and cryptographic algorithms. The performance is evaluated in terms of efficiency and practicality of our scheme. To be fair, for each experiment, we run it 10 times and take the average.

6.1 Parameters l_k and l_v

The process for encapsulating one ciphertext block G_i includes two main steps: (1) generating the lookup table T_i, and (2) transforming G_i to H_i with T_i.

The generation of a lookup table incurs 2^{l_v} hash operations. Moreover, the size of the lookup table is about $(l_k + l_v) \cdot 2^{l_k} + l_v \cdot 2^{l_v}$ bits. As listed in Table 2, by using MD5, the time cost for generating a lookup table, as well as the storage overhead of the lookup table, is dominated by l_v. In order to ensure that our proposal can meet practical security requirements, the data encapsulation has to be sufficiently slow. To increase computational and storage overheads for a misbehaved cloud server, l_v should be as large as possible.

With the fixed size of G, the transformation from G to H incurs $\frac{|G|}{l_k}$ memory accesses, thus the time complexity is inversely proportional to the value of l_k. Namely, the computational cost of transformation is higher with a smaller l_k, as shown in Fig. 2. Apparently, to make the transformation time required for a misbehaved cloud server be noticeable, l_k should be as small as possible. However, from the Fig. 3, we can see that small l_k leads to higher computational cost of data decapsulation. A main reason for this is that the decapsulation from H to G incurs $\frac{|G|}{l_k}$ hash operations. When the user wants to access some blocks of F, the time cost increases as l_k becomes smaller, which will in conflict with users' vision.

Besides, the additional storage cost introduced to an honest cloud server is about $|H| - |G|$, i.e., $\frac{l_v - l_k}{l_k}|G|$ since $|H| = \frac{l_v}{l_k}|G|$. The extra storage overhead rapidly grows in size with a larger l_v or a smaller l_k, which is not desired in this model.

Given the above consideration, it is important and necessary to set parameters l_k and l_v reasonably. In the proposed scheme, data users can tune these parameters to configure the slow process.

Table 2. The computational time and storage cost for a lookup table

l_k, l_v	16, 20	16, 24	16, 28	20, 24	20, 28	24, 28
Time cost (s)	0.29	5.06	86.64	5.23	90.77	94.19
Table size (MB)	2.75	48.32	896.35	53.80	902	1000

6.2 Theoretic Analysis

Table 3 compares our scheme with [15]. To make the comparison easier, we let n denote the number of all data blocks. Each block has m items. t is the number of challenged blocks among n blocks. C denotes the time cost of generating a lookup table. For communication overhead, we consider only the overhead at the phase of *Data Encapsualtion*. For cost of data updating, we consider only the computational cost at the user side. y is the number of challenged blocks among x updated blocks.

Note that in [15], the whole data encapsulation needs to be implemented by the resource-constrained user. However, in our scheme, it is conducted by the

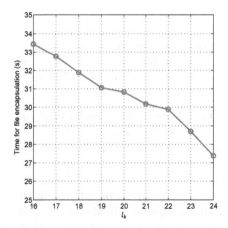 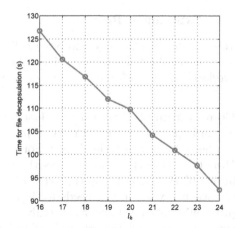

Fig. 2. The time cost for the transformation from G to H for the different l_k with the fixed size of G and l_v, $|G| = 1\,\mathrm{GB}$ and $l_v = 28$.

Fig. 3. The time cost for the transformation from H to G for the different l_k on a $\frac{l_v}{l_k}\mathrm{GB}$ file with the fixed l_v, $l_v = 28$.

cloud server, and the user only needs to do a small amount of computation. We remark that our scheme outperforms [15] in respect of communication overhead during data encapsulation. Our scheme is practical and secure against the cloud server, but at the price of requiring more interaction times (comparable with the interaction times required by [15]). It is worth mentioning that our solution is more efficient in terms of the cost for small data updates.

Table 3. The comparison between our scheme and [15].

Properties	Hu et al. [15]	Our scheme
Client computation	$O(n)\ C + O(nm)$ memory access	$O(t)\ C + O(tm)$ memory access
Server computation	–	$O(n)\ C + O(nm)$ memory access
Communication overhead	$|H|$	$|F|$
Interaction times	1	3
Cost of updating x blocks	$O(x)\ C + O(xm)$ memory access	$O(y)\ C + O(ym)$ memory access
Server storage	$O(n)$	$O(n)$
Client storage	$O(1)$	$O(1)$

6.3 Experiment Result

To evaluate the efficiency and practicality for data encryption verification task, we mainly adopt the computational cost at the user side and communication overhead as the performance metrics, which are presented in detail as follow.

Computational Cost on the User. At the phase of *Data Encapsulation*, in the implementation of the Hu's proposal, data encapsulation is conducted by the resource-constrained user. For n blocks of F, data encapsulation takes $O(n)$ $C + O(nm)$ memory access time, where m is the number of data items in one block and C is the time cost of generating a lookup table. However, in our scheme, what a user needs to do is to ensure that I_H is correct with high probability by challenging t randomly chosen blocks. Specifically, the user would conduct t encapsulation operations and generate t hash values. It means that I_H is correctly formatted if these hash values match corresponding values in I_H which is returned by the cloud server. Thus, the user-side computational cost in our scheme is $O(t)$ $C + O(tm)$ memory access time.

With assuming the cloud server just cheats on a tiny part of H, such as d blocks handled falsely among n blocks, and the cheating rate r is equal to $\frac{d}{n}$. We let P be the probability that at least one of the blocks cheated by the cloud matches one of the blocks picked by the user as below:

$$P = 1 - \frac{n-d}{n} \cdot \frac{n-d-1}{n-1} \cdots \frac{n-d-t+1}{n-t+1}. \tag{3}$$

Since $\frac{n-d}{n} \geq \frac{n-d-1}{n-1}$, so $1 - (\frac{n-d-t+1}{n-t+1})^t \geq P \geq 1 - (\frac{n-d}{n})^t$. As shown in Fig. 4, the experimental result proves that the probability P roughly increases logarithmically as the number t of challenged blocks increases. With the fixed number of file blocks ($n = 10000$), when the cheating rate is 0.5%, 1%, 5% and 10% respectively, provided that the number t of challenged blocks is more than 1287, 664, 133 and 65 respectively, the probability P would exceed 99.9%. In this case, the user-side computational cost in our proposal is 12.87%, 6.64%, 1.33% and 0.65% of that in [15].

According to the analysis in Sect. 6.1, we choose $l_k = 24$ and $l_v = 28$ in the implementation of the experiments. We divide all the files outsourced by the user into 100 blocks. According to the Eq. (3), when the cloud server cheats on 10% of H, the probability of cloud misbehavior detection exceeds 99%, as long as the user verifies any 35% of all the data blocks. In this setting, Fig. 5 gives the time cost at the user side of our scheme with that of Hu et al. [15] for different sizes of all files. The result shows, compared with [15], 65% of its computational cost on the user side is decreased in our scheme.

Computational Cost on the Server. Compared with [15], the cloud server in our proposed design needs to implement data encryption and encapsulation. Although the time cost on the server is a non-ignorable overhead, it is worth mentioning that it is executed only once.

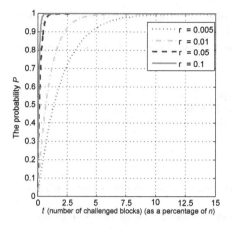
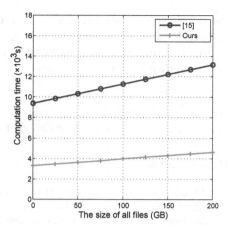

Fig. 4. The probability P for detecting the cloud server that fails to implement the transformation from F to H. We show P as a function of t (the number of blocks challenged by the user, shown as a percentage of n) for different values of cheating rate r with a fixed number of file blocks, $n = 10000$.

Fig. 5. Comparison of the computation time at the user side of our scheme with that of [15].

Communication Overhead. Compared with [15], our scheme needs to take up extra network bandwidth to transmit hash values I_H, instead of $|H| - |F| = \frac{l_v - l_k}{l_k}|F|$ communication consumption to upload H in [15]. In order to more clearly understand the difference between them, suppose that 1 GB data F is divided into 1000 blocks with $l_k = 24$ and $l_v = 28$. Then the size of each element in I_H is 128 bits by using MD5. The storage space of I_H is thus 15.625 KB. However, the extra communication overhead in [15] is 170.7 MB. It shows that there are significant cost savings for users to adopt our proposed scheme.

To sum up, our scheme could help to enhance users' experience and boost the practicability by bringing significant cost savings to users without impacting security.

7   Conclusion and Future Work

In this paper, we explored the problem of verifying if the cloud server ensures confidentiality protection for users' sensitive data. Our scheme enables the detection of cloud servers which fail to correctly store the data encrypted at rest. Our proposal brings significant cost savings to a user by introducing the pseudo-random number generator into data encapsulation. The high practicality makes our scheme well suited for resource-constrained users with lightweight computing devices. In addition, a pivotal component of our proposal is verifiable tags, which allow remote users to verify the actually deployed security measures by the cloud server. Extensive experimental results demonstrate the performance and practicality of our proposed scheme.

In our future work, we will focus on the methodologies with lower communication overhead during verification.

Acknowledgments. This research was supported by National Key Research and Development Program of China (Grant No. 2017YFB0802404) and partially supported by National Natural Science Foundation of China (Award No. 61772518).

References

1. Alibaba Cloud. https://www.alibabacloud.com/help/doc-detail/67829.htm?spm=a2c63.p38356.a1.3.3f341fecRxYbAx
2. Amazon S3. https://docs.aws.amazon.com/AmazonS3/latest/dev/UsingEncryption.html
3. Microsoft Azure. https://docs.microsoft.com/zh-cn/azure/security/security-azure-encryption-overview
4. OpenSSL. https://www.openssl.org/
5. RedLock: Cloud security trends, May 2018 Edition. https://info.redlock.io/cloud-security-trends-may2018?utm_source=website%20direct&utm_medium=feb2018
6. Alkhojandi, N., Miri, A.: Privacy-preserving public auditing in cloud computing with data deduplication. In: Cuppens, F., Garcia-Alfaro, J., Zincir Heywood, N., Fong, P.W.L. (eds.) FPS 2014. LNCS, vol. 8930, pp. 35–48. Springer, Cham (2015). https://doi.org/10.1007/978-3-319-17040-4_3
7. Armknecht, F., Barman, L., Bohli, J.M., et al.: Mirror: enabling proofs of data replication and retrievability in the cloud. In: 25th USENIX Security Symposium (USENIX Security 2016), pp. 1051–1068. USENIX Association, Austin (2016)
8. Armknecht, F., Bohli, J.M., Froelicher, D., et al.: Sport: Sharing proofs of retrievability across tenants. Cryptology ePrint Archive, Report 2016/724 (2016)
9. Ateniese, G., Burns, R., Curtmola, R., et al.: Provable data possession at untrusted stores. In: ACM Conference on Computer and Communications Security, pp. 598–609 (2007)
10. Benson, K., Dowsley, R., Shacham, H.: Do you know where your cloud files are? In: ACM Cloud Computing Security Workshop, Ccsw 2011, Chicago, IL, USA, pp. 73–82, October 2011
11. Bowers, K.D., Dijk, M.V., Juels, A., et al.: How to tell if your cloud files are vulnerable to drive crashes. In: ACM Conference on Computer and Communications Security, CCS 2011, Chicago, Illinois, USA, pp. 501–514, October 2011
12. van Dijk, M., Juels, A., Oprea, A., et al.: Hourglass schemes: how to prove that cloud files are encrypted, pp. 265–280 (2012)
13. Fu, A., Yu, S., Zhang, Y., et al.: NPP: a new privacy-aware public auditing scheme for cloud data sharing with group users. IEEE Trans. Big Data 1 (2017)
14. Gorke, C.A., Janson, C., Armknecht, F., et al.: Cloud storage file recoverability. In: ACM International Workshop on Security in Cloud Computing (2017)
15. Hu, K., Zhang, W.: Efficient verification of data encryption on cloud servers. In: Twelfth International Conference on Privacy, Security and Trust, pp. 314–321 (2014)
16. Hur, J., Koo, D., Shin, Y., et al.: Secure data deduplication with dynamic ownership management in cloud storage. IEEE Trans. Knowl. Data Eng. **28**(11), 3113–3125 (2016)

17. Juels, A.: PORs: proofs of retrievability for large files. In: ACM Conference on Computer and Communications Security, pp. 584–597 (2007)
18. Li, D., Chen, J., Guo, C., et al.: IP-geolocation mapping for moderately connected internet regions. IEEE Trans. Parallel Distrib. Syst. **24**(2), 381–391 (2013)
19. Li, J., Li, J., Xie, D., et al.: Secure auditing and deduplicating data in cloud. IEEE Trans. Comput. **65**(8), 2386–2396 (2016)
20. Long, M., Li, Y., Peng, F.: Dynamic provable data possession of multiple copies in cloud storage based on full-node of AVL tree. Int. J. Digit. Crime Forensics **11**(1), 126–137 (2019)
21. Shen, W., Qin, J., Yu, J., et al.: Enabling identity-based integrity auditing and data sharing with sensitive information hiding for secure cloud storage. IEEE Trans. Inf. Forensics Secur. **14**(2), 331–346 (2019)
22. Wang, B., Li, B., Li, H.: Panda: public auditing for shared data with efficient user revocation in the cloud. IEEE Trans. Serv. Comput. **8**(1), 92–106 (2015)
23. Wang, Q., Ren, K., Lou, W., et al.: Dependable and secure sensor data storage with dynamic integrity assurance. In: INFOCOM, pp. 954–962 (2009)
24. Wang, Q., Wang, C., Ren, K., et al.: Enabling public auditability and data dynamics for storage security in cloud computing. IEEE Trans. Parallel Distrib. Syst. **22**(5), 847–859 (2011)
25. Wang, Z., Sun, K., Jing, J., et al.: Verification of data redundancy in cloud storage. In: Proceedings of the 2013 international workshop on Security in cloud computing, pp. 11–18 (2013)
26. Wu, Y., Jiang, Z.L., Wang, X., et al.: Dynamic data operations with deduplication in privacy-preserving public auditing for secure cloud storage. In: IEEE International Conference on Computational Science and Engineering, pp. 562–567 (2017)
27. Yang, G., Yu, J., Shen, W., et al.: Enabling public auditing for shared data in cloud storage supporting identity privacy and traceability. J. Syst. Softw. **113**, 130–139 (2016)

Generating Personalized and Certifiable Workflow Designs: A Prototype

Manon Froger[1,2(✉)], Frederick Bénaben[1], Sébastien Truptil[1],
and Nicolas Boissel-Dallier[2]

[1] Ecole des Mines d'Albi, Campus Jarlard, 81013 Albi Cedex 09, France
{manon.froger, frederick.benaben,
sebastien.truptil}@mines-albi.fr
[2] Iterop, 1B rue Antoine Lavoisier, Colomiers 31770, France
{mfroger, nboissel}@iterop.com

Abstract. As the first level of a BPM strategy, being able to design event-oriented models of processes is a must-have competence for every modern business. Unfortunately, industrial procedures have reached a certain complexity making the designing task complex enough to discourage businesses facing the blank page. Moreover, the 21st century witnesses the emergence of myriads of norms and external regulations that businesses want to abide by. Although domain experts have a limited process modelling and norm interpretation knowledge, they know how to describe their activities and their sequencing. With progresses made in the artificial intelligence, particularly in the natural language processing domain, it becomes possible to automatize the task of creating a process in compliance with norms. This paper presents a business-oriented prototype assisting users in getting certifiable specific business processes. We detail the metamodel used to separately model norms and business' existing procedures and then, the algorithm envisaged to deduce a corresponding cartography of processes.

Keywords: Cartography generation · Design compliance · Workflow design · Business alignment

1 Introduction

In an era where certifications are a pledge of quality for every stakeholder [1], industries are increasingly heading towards having their processes orchestrated [2]. Business Process Management Suites (BPMS) aim to meet this requirement by providing a platform to run models designed beforehand [3]. Process modelling is an expensive, time-consuming but essential step before being able to run a process [4]. Despite the help provided by new graphical modelling tools integrated into process design software products (Process Mining [5], Correctness and Compliance checking [6]) the learning curve is still too slow [7].

Business processes are usually computerized for three reasons [8]: having a continuous improvement approach, getting certified, and conciliating computer systems with the organization's inner operations. Remaining competitive and getting certifications

J. E. Ferreira et al. (Eds.): SCC 2019, LNCS 11515, pp. 32–47, 2019.
https://doi.org/10.1007/978-3-030-23554-3_3

mainly caused companies' processes to reach a certain level of complexity making the modeling stage too complex to be made by anyone [9], like it used to be and should probably remain. Industries need guidance to design their processes.

Business Process Model and Notation (BPMN) editors have long been used for designing process only, and thus haven't been conceived to speed up process orchestration procedure [7]. BPMS need a functionality to think differently the BPM strategy and to systematically provide certifiable, easily modifiable and computerizable processes. A solution to make process modelling intuitive and accessible is becoming primordial.

Making modelling easier implies on the one hand supporting the designing stage with methods simple enough to be understandable by any novice and on the other hand complex enough to respond to a large variety of business problems. These methods should avoid the modeler from making both syntactical (i.e. grammatically incorrect) and semantical (i.e. logically or spelling incorrect) mistakes. Although a variety of researches [10] on the computer-aided design of processes have been conducted, very few have focused on automatically generating part of processes except for [11–14] which all constitutes the grounding of the presented work. Our Research tries to improve them by defining an assistant able to facilitate the design of processes

Use Case. Our work aims at conceiving an assistant to automatically generate a business process cartography for users with already defined procedures and wanting to abide by rules identified beforehand. Iterop[1] provides the use case that will guide this article: an Aircraft Supplying Company aiming at complying with the ISO 15288:2015 certification [15]. This use case illustrates each of the following section of the article.

Section 2 of this paper presents existing solutions for design-time assistance. Section 3 details our approach to assist users in designing their compliant processes: (1) how to model business' existing procedures and norms requirements (Sect. 3.1), how to acknowledge similarities between business and norms terms (Sect. 3.2), how to finally deduce compliant specific business processes (Sect. 3.3). Section 4 finally exposes our prototype's limitations and raises some research perspectives.

2 Related Work and Positioning

A process is a collection of tasks structured to achieve one or more specific goal [16]. With the growing number of companies having a full BPM strategy since the 1990's, process designing quickly became a core research subject [17]. SemTechBPM (Semantic Technology in Business Process Modeling) has been established to be a common ground for discussion about BPM conception and modelling. In [18], they outline different research streams in assisting modelling. Among them, **correctness and compliance checking** consist in validating technical properties of models, such as the absence of deadlocks. This method does not "assist" modelling as it takes part at the

---

[1] Iterop is a French small company developing a BPMS: IteropSuite. Most of its clients provides their existing procedures and expect a matching cartography in return. As for now, cartography are thought by BPM experts.

end of the modelling-time. Nevertheless, it does prevent from making syntactical mistakes.

In 2007, a **syntax-based user assistance** in diagram editors DiaGen has been released to support medical diagram designing with an auto-completion feature. [19] describes how this approach can be applied to BPMN language. The resulting functionality would offer an automatic completion to partially designed processes and correctness-preserving editing operations. This method can help to preserve model's syntactic correctness and ease process modelling. [20] provides the description and use case of 20 workflow patterns that can be used for completion: from the basic sequence to the complex interleaved parallel routing. Although, as detailed in [21], one can say that the workflow patterns do not appear to be 'suitable' for satisfactory business process model descriptions, this method has proved its applicability as it has already been integrated to editors as presented in [22]. [23] also identifies several types of recommendation from structural to name completion.

Moreover, in the last decade, researchers have exploited this feature to also preserve semantic compliance by completing their being-modelled process with part of others as detailed in [24]. Actually, due to the endless number of process models designed to respond to very specific problematics, reusing them as part of models recommended during the design-time would strongly support users facing the writer's block. [25] proposes a first algorithm for discovering and analyzing activity pattern co-occurrences in business process models. [26, 27] both demonstrate the applicability of the extraction of patterns by presenting a set of patterns extracted from a set of models. Besides, these patterns are both necessary and enough to design all processes that were investigated proving how process patterns can support process modelers in generating new models. These parts of model can be stored in a repository and then be found using tags describing the goal of the process as proposed in [7]. Although the benefits of this solution seem obvious, **business process reuse** is not commonly used. As outlined in [28], this lack of enthusiasm is first due to the poor support for process model reuse but also to the lack of knowledge of what could be achieved with this feature.

In 2000, [29] presented an adaptation of robotics and military logistics based on AI techniques (artificial intelligence) for the domain of workflow engines. For example, **process mining** has proven its utility by using business events logs to generate processes. Yet, many researchers have developed powerful process mining techniques, but very few of them had been tested on real-life processes before [30], and still today, very few of these techniques are integrated to support process designing. Despite the evident industrial applicability, industries aiming at designing theirs processes in a certification purpose still lack modeling knowledge to improve generated processes.

Use Case. Our use case's company does not have any processes designed yet, and thus does not store any logs. Process Mining and Correctness and Compliance Checking functionalities cannot help them in getting theirs processes designed. Syntax-based user assistance functionalities would help them in getting specific business processes but would not assist them in merging norm requirements. Conversely, Business Process Reuse tools would help in enriching processes with norm requirements however would only results in generic business processes. We wish to generate processes which are not specific and compliant with desired norms.

Since 2000's, workflow design has become a subject of interest and various IT supporting tools have been developed to assist user during process modeling. However, existing tools rarely help users facing a blank page and not familiar with process modeling languages and methods. Researches should deal with the subject in depth as it constitutes a real answer for continuous improvement issues. The emergence of artificial intelligence raises the possibility of helping users during their process modeling by generating process cartography, not only corresponding to existing procedures but also abiding by desired rules. Such a functionality should not be based on using event logs but on collecting existing procedures information in a user-friendly method. Next section presents our conception of a modelling assistant based on procedures described by users using a business-oriented language (composed of functions, data, and relative positioning notions), to generate a business process cartography.

3   Toward an Assistant Supporting Process Design

The 21st century marked the beginning of the growing interest of the scientific community in compliance problems. Notions of Agility, Usability, Scalability, Strategies and Norm Modeling quickly populates the Business Process Compliance Space [17]. Our desire is to develop a functionality automatizing process generation using the less human intervention as possible. Therefore, we aim at computerizing most of what is usually manually performed: (1) gathering generic process exigences to enforce rules, (2) interviewing process stakeholders to gather information about existing procedures, (3) getting the set of rules that the resulting cartography should abide by, (4) improving cartography with rules interpretations to ensure resulting processes compliance. Figure 1 pictures a IDEF-0 representation of the desired functionality.

To generate a cartography complying with procedures described by a business and abiding by rules preselected by the business, we identified three scientific challenges and detail them in upcoming subsections: (i) how should we represent parts of processes coming from both businesses and norms (Sect. 3.1), (ii) how can we identify where norm process parts should participate in the cartography (Sect. 3.2), (iii) how can processes be generated from both business and norm inputs (Sect. 3.3).

3.1   Input Formalization Language

Our approach requires that we first gather information coming from both business and norms. Norm exigences are rules our cartography should abide by, and we decided to also consider business exigences as rules to comply with.

A business rule is a statement that defines or constrains some aspect of the business. It is intended to assert business structure or to control or influence the behavior of the business [31]. Compliance measures are very abstract specifications [32], documented and communicated in natural language. Therefore, conceiving a compliance measures description meta-model constitutes the first challenge of the presented work. 1st paragraph of this section summarizes concepts coming along with rule description. 2nd paragraph details how we decided to capitalize exigences coming from both norms and businesses, Fig. 2 pictures its UML representation.

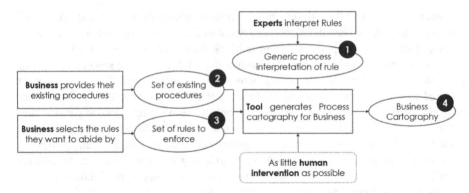

Fig. 1. Structured analysis and design technique (IDEF-0) model of the prototype

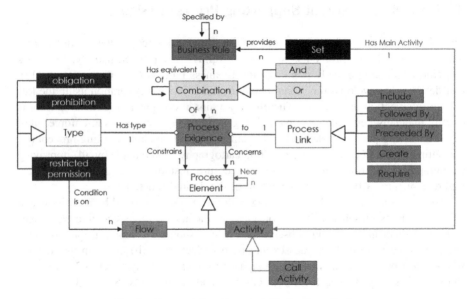

Fig. 2. Metamodel used to describe Business Rules

Literature Review Around Rule Description. According to [17], compliance problems are divided into five categories: (1) design-time, (2) run-time and (3) hybrid
approaches, (4) auditing and (5) organizational and internal control frameworks. The
strategy of the presented work is to focus on (1) design-time compliance issues. [33]
considers two main types for formal model of compliance requirements: temporal logic
approaches (i.e. specified formally with temporal logic formulas [34] such as BPMN-Q
[35], BPSL [36] and DecSerFlow [37]) and deontic logic approaches (i.e. normative
concepts such as obligations, permissions, prohibitions and related notions [38] such as
Business Contract Language [39] or Process ENtailment from the ELicitation of
Obligations and PErmission [40]). [41] defines the three kinds of statement to express
operative business rules: (1) obligation statement (i.e. declaration that should be true

but can be violated and must be enforced), (2) prohibition statement (i.e. what should not be, by policy) and (3) restricted permission statement (i.e. what is permitted in certain condition). [42] explains that expressing sequences of activities and conditional execution are enough in terms of expressing control flow. Thus, a model to describe Businesses' existing procedures should allow the use of notions such as conditions, inclusion, relative occurrence of activities, provision and usage of data.

[43] proves that temporal logic is not suitable alone to model norms and legal reasoning and [44] demonstrates that deontic logic does not provide suitable logical tools to account for legal phenomena like enactment, derogation, and conflicts between legal norms which rely on systemic legal validity. Therefore, a valid model for compliance requirements should both integrate temporal and logical notions. [45] raises the principle of Declarative Modeling and [46] investigates the feasibility of using common vocabulary to integrate compliance rules. Our envisaged structure is based on this idea.

Envisaged Model. Our research believes that a *Business Rule* is a declaration always defined using a natural language (i.e. simple sentences) and that a *Business Rule* can always contains and *be specified by* other *Business Rules*. For instance, "The organization shall plan and control the design and development of product" is specified by "During the design and development planning, the organization shall determine the design and development stages". In order to unforce process compliance, *Business Rules* must then be converted in an equivalent *Combination* of *Process Exigences*. Thus, a process can be checked or modified to abide by the *Business Rule*. Each *Process Exigence* has one of the three existing *types* of Rules: *obligation*, *prohibition* or *restricted permission*.

A *Process Exigence* defines a positioning (inclusion, relative occurrence, provision, usage) between *Process Elements* (*Flow*, *Activity*). We needed to add connections *Near* and *Has Main Activity*, for the next phase of our developments. We explain them in Sects. 3.2 and 3.3). Section 4.1 presents the technology we choose to use to implement models.

Use Case. Our use case's company wishes to follow the Iso 15288 guidelines. ISO/IEC/IEEE 15288 is an international standard providing generic process descriptions and requirements [47]. One of the rules detailed in the ISO/IEC/IEEE 15288 certification states: "Main Activity should include an activity named "supply process" and an activity named "maintenance process". Experts can translate this rule into a process exigence: "Main Activity is obliged to include an activity named "supply process" and an activity named "implementation process"". Figure 3 pictures this interpretation of the rule using previously described meta model. Using our metamodel, experts can interpret the entire ISO 15288 certification and our use case's company is able to develop its internal procedures. Next Section is dedicated to adding the "Near" links between Process Elements.

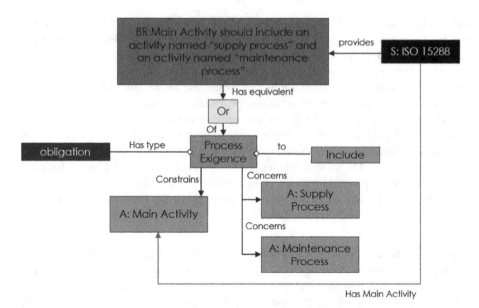

Fig. 3. Model for Business Rule "Main Activity is obliged to include an activity named "supply process" and an activity named "maintenance process"."

3.2   Similarity Links

Our research believes that existing procedures should be the foundation of the generated cartography. In order to correctly feed this foundation with the requirements of the selected norms, it is primordial to measure resemblance between business and norms inputs. This section details the necessity to detect matching terms and then the method we use to find them. This equivalence would be registered by linking two *Process Elements* thanks to a *Near* connection (see the *Near* link in Fig. 2).

Use Case. *Our use case's company decided to only detail its core activity: Supply. When enforcing the ISO-15288 rule, it is important to add an activity "Maintenance Process" as stated in the norm. But it is also important to not add and activity "Supply Process" since it already exists. In a situation where Process Elements are recognized as equivalent, the generated cartography: (1) must not contain duplicates, (2) should prefer business inputs to norm inputs.*

Multiple Case for Similarity. Figure 4 represents a generic example of a Business Input, a Norm Input and the expected resulting cartography. This example shows the cartography expected depending on business inputs, norm inputs and identified similarities.

In this example, a business provides the following information: "Our main activity includes activities A, B1, B2, C1 and C2", a norm provides the following rules: "Main Activity should include activities A, B and C. Activity A should include activities A1 and A2. Activity B should include activities B1 and B2. Activity C should include activities C1, C2 and C3".

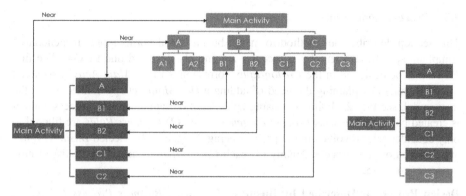

Fig. 4. Cartography generated (on the right) corresponding to the union of Business input (green) and a Norm input (orange). (Color figure online)

In the generated cartography, the business input is kept as original, and norm activities can be added. Activity A should not be added since it already exists. Activity B does not have to be added since it is entirely represented by activities B1 and B2. Activity C can't be added because it is already partially represented by activities C1 and C2, however, to entirely represent required activity C, activity C3 needs to be added.

Existing Tools and Comparison. Semantic similarity is a measure representing a distance between a set of documents or terms, based on the likeness of their meaning. Measures of similarity between words or concepts have been widely explored for the past two decades, over multiple domains of application [48–52] and various tools and algorithm have been developed.

For our use of a semantic similarity detection tool, we can see the functionality as a recommendation system. We decided to compare existing tools thanks to the measure of indicators inspired from statistical analysis. We first built a reference of binary responses (expected similar or not) between 30 Norm terms and 20 Business terms. We gathered the 600 similarity scores given by each algorithm and tool in our possession (ElasticSearch, spaCy, Wikibrain, UMBC, Optimal Matching, Greedy Pairing, MCS method, LSA, Snips, DKPro Similarity, Similarity Search Java, NGD, ESA, SimRank). For each table of results, we defined a frontier to convert percentages into binary response (evaluated similar or not).

For our use of the tool, we decided to compare tools against two measures; (1) the false positive rate (FPR) (also known as the Fall-out or probability of false alarm) and the (2) true positive rate (TPR) (also known as the Recall, Sensitivity or probability of detection). Section 4.1 presents the technology we choose to use.

$$\text{FPR} = \frac{\Sigma \text{ False Positives}}{\Sigma \text{ Expected Negatives}} \tag{1}$$

$$\text{TPR} = \frac{\Sigma \text{ True Positives}}{\Sigma \text{ Expected Positives}} \tag{2}$$

3.3   Process Generation

This section describes our method to merge business and norms inputs to generate a compliant specific cartography. *Processes* are entirely designed one by one. The first *Process* to be designed in the *Cartography* corresponds to the *Main Activity* declared by the Business (explaining the need of adding a *Has Main activity* connection in the metamodel, see Fig. 2). Following paragraphs detail our approach: (1) Process content is created based on business *Process Exigences* only, (2) *Business Rules* are filtered to only consider rules involved in the process being designed, (3) selected *Business Rules* are enforced on this process. Finally (4) each *Call Activity* is added to the list of next processes to write.

Design Process as Described by Business. Following *Business Process Exigences*, we identify every *activity* that must be in the process. Every time an activity is added to the process we check if its neighbors are already added to the process (otherwise we need to create them) and create a relational link in-between. Process is entirely described using relational notions (such as conditions, inclusion, relative occurrence of activities, provision and usage of data). We developed a methodology to deduce a BPMN Model based on these relations which is detailed in an internal report [53]. This paper is only dedicated to detail how we obtain the relations.

Business Rules are Filtered. *Process Exigences* coming Norms are filtered to only implies those concerned by the *Process*. The filtering operates by keeping only Exigences concerned by desired *Process*. It first gets existing *Process Elements* in the *Process* and every connected *Near Process Element*. An *Exigence* is considered as "involved" if (1) it has an *Include* type and *concerns* the *Process Main Activity* or if (2) it has not an *Include* type and *concerns* one of the *Process Elements* in the *Process* or their *Nears*.

Business Rules are Enforced on the Process. Process *Exigences* are consecutively enforced on the process using the EnforceProcessExigence described below. Every time a new *Process Element* is added to the process, newly involved rules are added to the list of *Process Exigences* to Enforce. The following algorithm describes the EnforceProcessExigence function which requires the *Process Exigence* to enforce, the *Process* to modify, and a list of every *Process Exigences(allconstraints)* coming from Business and Norms.

```
Function EnforceProcessExigence
   exigence: Process Exigence
   process: Process
   allconstraints:[ProcessExigence]

Begin
     elementToAppear <- getElementToAppear(exigence)
     activitiesInProcess <- getAllActivitiesAnd-
     Nears(process)

   if activitiesInProcess NOT contains elementToAppear

       AscendanceOfElementToAppear <- getAscend-
       ance(elementToAppear, allconstraints)

       appearingAscendance<- activitiesInProcess UNION
       AscendanceOfElementToAppear

     if appearingAscendance is empty

         requiredElementsToAppear <- getElementsToAp-
         pear(elementToAppear, process, activitiesInPro-
         cess, allconstraints)

         For each childElementToAppear in requiredEle-
         mentsToAppear
           If activitiesInProcess NOT contains childEle-
           mentToAppear

             Process.add(childElementToAppear)

           End if
         end for
       end if
     end if
  End
```

The getElementToAppear function returns *Process Elements concerned* by *Process Exigence*. The getAscendance and getDescendance functions return *Process Elements* linked to a desired *Process Element* through *allconstraints* thanks to *Include*, *Followed By* and *Preceded By* links.

The getElementsToAppear function returns only *Process Elements* to appear. Starting with *ElementToAppear*, if getDescendance UNION *activitiesInProcess* contains something, *ElementToAppear* is replaced by its immediate descendance. This procedure is repeated until descendance of all *ElementsToAppear* is not already in *activitiesInProcess*. Thus, the function adds to *Process* the "higher" activity of each not yet represented Activity.

Finish Process and Select Next Processes to be Designed. Once the *Process* is finished, it is added to the *Cartography*. If added *activities* should also include other *activities*, type is set to *Call Activities* and *activities* are added to the list of next *Processes* to be written.

Use Case. Figure 5 displays the BPMN Model of the Supply Process obtained for our use case's Company. Top of the Figure shows the Model as described by business only. Bottom of the Figure pictures to the same model enriched with ISO:15288 exigences. The four green-unlighted activities in bottom process correspond to required activities with no equivalent found in the process, they have been added next to their neighbors' equivalent.

4   Conclusion

4.1   Preliminary Results

A prototype is being developed, combining functionalities for (1) model creation, (2) similarities detection and (3) cartography generation.

Concerning the meta model detailed Sect. 3.1, since a *Business Rule* can always be specified by another *Business Rule*, and because every *Business Rule* is then converted into *Combinations* of *Process Exigences*, implying varying *Flow Elements*, our models might reach an infinite depth we needed to deal with. We decided to represent our models using a graph database with an Apache 2.0 License and an existing Java client: Orient DB. Figure 6 shows a screen shot of the implemented graph database.

For similarity detection functionality explained in Sect. 3.2, we chose to use a reconciliation tool with an Apache License and an available Java API, a FPR lower than 30% and a TPR higher than 15%. ElasticSearch verify these conditions. Completed with a synonym token filter based on wordnet synonyms [54], results obtained with Elastic search are even higher. We are also investigating the use of neural network-based functionalities to deal with similarity detection.

We are currently implementing our process generation algorithm in a Java application, and we can generate cartography for simple case such as the one in our use case, Fig. 5 is a screen shot of what our application generated for our use case with and without norms selected.

4.2   Limitations and Perspectives

Design-time compliance approaches have slightly less been investigated than run-time approaches since 2000 [17]. Since compliance has been recognized as a NP-complete problem [17] there is no known way to find a solution quickly. We chose to improve an existing process (given by a Business) by enforcing consecutives Process Exigences in order.

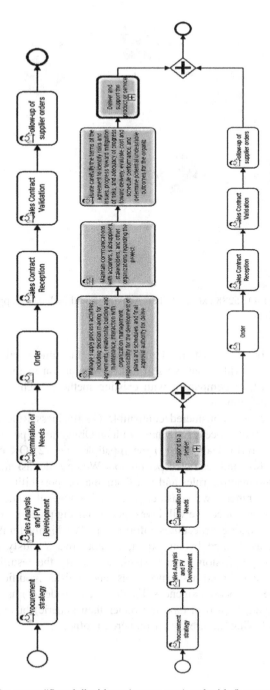

Fig. 5. Business Processes "Supply" without (top process) and with (bottom process) norm ISO-15288 selected

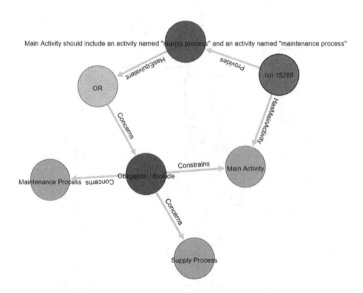

Fig. 6. Model of as ISO 15288 extract: "Main Activity should include a Supply Process and an Implementation Process"

We think that our IT assistance highly reduces the time needed to generate a cartography abiding by rules, but we still lack an evaluation method to validate our prototype or, at least, to compare it with existing methods such as manual process conception or process mining.

As for now, we only considered compatible (1) Business Rules, converted into AND combination (2) of Process Exigences with an Obligation type (3). Our prototype is then missing a way to deal with (1) incompatible rule, (2) OR combination and (3) types of prohibition and restricted permission. We consider asking the business to choose between incompatible rules and OR Combination possibility.

For future development, we consider taking advantage of some of the methods raised in Sect. 2. For instance, we will investigate (1) using process mining techniques to gather business existing procedures information. We highly think that a generic Process Exigence, as defined by an expert, cannot always satisfy Businesses. We consider giving the permission for a business to modify the resulting cartography, supported by (2) syntax-based assistance tools, and register modification as specific alternatives of generic process exigences. Finally, we consider (3) using process reuse techniques to generate improved (specific rather than generic) business process cartography for users having an already encountered profile.

References

1. Baker, S.W.: Formalizing agility, part 2: how an agile organization embraced the CMMI. In: AGILE 2006 (AGILE 2006), July 2006
2. van der Aalst, W.M.P.: Business process management: a comprehensive survey. ISRN Softw. Eng. **2013**, 1–37 (2013). https://doi.org/10.1155/2013/507984
3. Meidan, A., García-García, J.A., Escalona, M.J., Ramos, I.: A survey on business processes management suites. Comput. Stand. Interfaces. **51**, 71–86 (2017)
4. Claes, J., Vanderfeesten, I., Pinggera, J., Reijers, H.A., Weber, B., Poels, G.: A visual analysis of the process of process modeling. Inf. Syst. E-Bus. Manag. **13**, 147–190 (2015). https://doi.org/10.1007/s10257-014-0245-4
5. van der Aalst, W.: Process mining: data science in action (2016)
6. Dumas, M., Rosa, M.L., Mendling, J., Reijers, H.A.: Fundamentals of business process management. Fundam. Bus. Process Manag. **1**, 2 (2013)
7. Hornung, T., Koschmider, A., Lausen, G.: Recommendation based process modeling support: method and user experience. In: Li, Q., Spaccapietra, S., Yu, E., Olivé, A. (eds.) ER 2008. LNCS, vol. 5231, pp. 265–278. Springer, Heidelberg (2008). https://doi.org/10.1007/978-3-540-87877-3_20
8. Benaben, F., Mu, W., Boissel-Dallier, N., Barthe-Delanoe, A.-M., Zribi, S., Pingaud, H.: Supporting interoperability of collaborative networks through engineering of a service-based Mediation Information System (MISE 2.0). Enterp. Inf. Syst., 1–27 (2014). https://doi.org/10.1080/17517575.2014.928949
9. Vernadat, F.: Enterprise modeling and integration (1996)
10. Fellmann, M., Zarvic, N., Sudau, A.: Ontology-based assistance for semi-formal process modeling, pp. 117–132 (2013)
11. Rajsiri, V., Lorré, J.-P., Benaben, F., Pingaud, H.: Knowledge-based system for collaborative process specification. Comput. Ind. **61**, 161–175 (2010)
12. Truptil, S.: Etude de l'approche de l'interopérabilité par médiation dans le cadre d'une dynamique de collaboration appliquée à la gestion de crise (2011)
13. Mu, W.: Caractérisation et logique d'une situation collaborative (2012)
14. Montarnal, A.: Deduction of inter-organizational collaborative business processes within an enterprise social network (2015)
15. International Organization for Standardization: ISO/IEC/IEEE 15288:2015. https://www.iso.org/standard/63711.html
16. Ko, R.K.L.: A computer scientist's introductory guide to business process management (BPM). Crossroads **15**, 11–18 (2009). https://doi.org/10.1145/1558897.1558901
17. Hashmi, M., Governatori, G., Lam, H.-P., Wynn, M.T.: Are we done with business process compliance: state of the art and challenges ahead. Knowl. Inf. Syst., 1–55 (2018). https://doi.org/10.1007/s10115-017-1142-1
18. Fellmann, M., Zarvic, N., Metzger, D., Koschmider, A.: Requirements catalog for business process modeling recommender systems, pp. 393–407 (2015)
19. Mazanek, S., Minas, M.: Business process models as a showcase for syntax-based assistance in diagram editors, pp. 322–336 (2009)
20. Aalst, W.M.P. van der, Hofstede, A.H.M., ter Kiepuszewski, B., Barros, A.P.: Workflow patterns. Encycl. Database Syst., 3557–3558 (2009). https://doi.org/10.1023/a:1022883727209
21. Börger, E.: Approaches to modeling business processes: a critical analysis of BPMN, workflow patterns and YAWL. Softw. Syst. Model. **11**, 305–318 (2012)

22. Koschmider, A., Hornung, T., Oberweis, A.: Recommendation-based editor for business process modeling. Data Knowl. Eng. **70**, 483–503 (2011). https://doi.org/10.1016/j.datak. 2011.02.002

23. Kluza, K., Baran, M., Bobek, S., Nalepa, G.: Overview of recommendation techniques in business process modeling. In: Proceedings 9th Workshop Knowledge Engineering and Software Engineering, KESE 9, pp. 46–57 (2013)

24. Fellmann, M., Koschmider, A., Schoknecht, A., Governance, C.: Analysis of business process model reuse literature: are research concepts empirically validated?, pp. 185–192 (2014)

25. Lau, J., Iochpe, C., Thom, L., Reichert, M.: Discovery and analysis of activity pattern cooccurrences in business process models (2009)

26. Koschmider, A., Reijers, H.A.: Improving the process of process modelling by the use of domain process patterns. Enterp. Inf. Syst. **9**, 29–57 (2013). https://doi.org/10.1080/ 17517575.2013.857792

27. Thom, L.: A pattern-based approach for business process modeling (2006)

28. Koschmider, A., Fellmann, M., Schoknecht, A., Oberweis, A.: Analysis of process model reuse: where are we now, where should we go from here? Decis. Support Syst. **66**, 9–19 (2014). https://doi.org/10.1016/j.dss.2014.05.012

29. R-Moreno, M.D., Borrajo, D., Meziat, D.: Process modelling and AI planning techniques: a new approach. In: Second International Workshop Information Integration and Web-Based Applications & Services, IIWAS 2000 (2000)

30. van der Aalst, W.M., Netjes, M., Reijers, H.A.: Supporting the full BPM life-cycle using process mining and intelligent redesign. In: Siau, K. (ed.) Contemporary Issues in Database Design and Information Systems Development, pp. 100–132 (2007)

31. El Kharbili, M., Stein, S., Markovic, I., Pulvermüller, E.: Towards a framework for semantic business process compliance management. In: Proceedings of GRCIS, vol. 2008. Citeseer (2008)

32. El Kharbili, M., Stein, S., Markovic, I., Pulvermüller, E.: Towards a framework for semantic business process compliance management. In: Proceedings GRCIS 2008 (2008)

33. Elgammal, A., Turetken, O., van den Heuvel, W.-J., Papazoglou, M.: Formalizing and applying compliance patterns for business process compliance. Softw. Syst. Model. **15**, 119–146 (2016). https://doi.org/10.1007/s10270-014-0395-3

34. Liu, Y., Muller, S., Xu, K.: A static compliance-checking framework for business process models. IBM Syst. J. **46**, 335–361 (2007). https://doi.org/10.1147/sj.462.0335

35. Awad, A., Decker, G., Weske, M.: Efficient compliance checking using BPMN-Q and temporal logic. In: Dumas, M., Reichert, M., Shan, M.-C. (eds.) BPM 2008. LNCS, vol. 5240, pp. 326–341. Springer, Heidelberg (2008). https://doi.org/10.1007/978-3-540-85758-7_24

36. Xu, K., Liu, Y., Wu, C.: BPSL modeler – visual notation language for intuitive business property reasoning. Electron. Notes Theor. Comput. Sci. **211**, 211–220 (2008). https://doi. org/10.1016/j.entcs.2008.04.043

37. van der Aalst, W.M.P., Pesic, M.: DecSerFlow: towards a truly declarative service flow language. In: Bravetti, M., Núñez, M., Zavattaro, G. (eds.) WS-FM 2006. LNCS, vol. 4184, pp. 1–23. Springer, Heidelberg (2006). https://doi.org/10.1007/11841197_1

38. Sadiq, S., Governatori, G., Namiri, K.: Modeling control objectives for business process compliance. In: Alonso, G., Dadam, P., Rosemann, M. (eds.) BPM 2007. LNCS, vol. 4714, pp. 149–164. Springer, Heidelberg (2007). https://doi.org/10.1007/978-3-540-75183-0_12

39. Governatori, G., Milosevic, Z.: A formal analysis of a business contract language. Int. J. Coop. Inf. Syst. **15**, 659–685 (2006). https://doi.org/10.1142/S0218843006001529

40. Goedertier, S., Vanthienen, J.: Designing compliant business processes with obligations and permissions. In: Eder, J., Dustdar, S. (eds.) BPM 2006. LNCS, vol. 4103, pp. 5–14. Springer, Heidelberg (2006). https://doi.org/10.1007/11837862_2

41. Hinkelmann, K.: SBVR-Semantics of Business Vocabulary and Business Rules

42. Weber, I., Paik, H.-Y., Benatallah, B., Vorwerk, C., Zheng, L., Kim, S.: Personal process management: design and execution for end-users (2010)

43. Governatori, G.: Thou Shalt is not You Will. ArXiv14041685 Cs (2014)

44. Mazzarese, T.: Deontic logic as logic of legal norms: two main sources of problems. Ratio Juris. **4**, 374–392 (1991). https://doi.org/10.1111/j.1467-9337.1991.tb00107.x

45. Goedertier, S., Vanthienen, J.: Declarative process modeling with business vocabulary and business rules. In: Meersman, R., Tari, Z., Herrero, P. (eds.) OTM 2007. LNCS, vol. 4805, pp. 603–612. Springer, Heidelberg (2007). https://doi.org/10.1007/978-3-540-76888-3_83

46. van der Aalst, W., van Hee, K., van der Werf, J.M., Kumar, A., Verdonk, M.: Conceptual model for online auditing. Decis. Support Syst. **50**, 636–647 (2011). https://doi.org/10.1016/j.dss.2010.08.014

47. Walden, D.D., Roedler, G.J., Forsberg, K., Hamelin, R.D., Shortell, T.M.: International Council on Systems Engineering. In: Systems Engineering Handbook: A Guide for System Life Cycle Processes and Activities. Wiley, Hoboken (2015)

48. Lin, D.: Automatic retrieval and clustering of similar words. In: 17th International Conference Computational Linguistics, vol. 2 (1998)

49. Budanitsky, A.: Lexical semantic relatedness and its application in natural language processing (1999)

50. Han, X., Zhao, J.: Structural semantic relatedness: a knowledge-based method to named entity disambiguation. In: Proceedings of the 48th Annual Meeting of the Association for Computational Linguistics, pp. 50–59. Association for Computational Linguistics, Uppsala (2010)

51. Zesch, T.: Study of semantic relatedness of words using collaboratively constructed semantic resources (2010). http://tuprints.ulb.tu-darmstadt.de/2041/1/PhD_TorstenZesch_SemanticRelatedness_2009.pdf

52. Wang, T.: A study to define an automatic model transformation approach based on semantic and syntactic comparisons (2016)

53. Froger, M.: Comment accompagner la modélisation des processus d'une entreprise ? Ecole Nationale des Mines D'Albi (2016)

54. Kuc, R., Rogozinski, M.: Elasticsearch Server. Packt Publishing Ltd. (2013)

An Empirical Investigation of Real-World QoS of Web Services

Yang Syu$^{(\boxtimes)}$ and Chien-Min Wang

Institute of Information Science, Academia Sinica, Taipei City, Taiwan (R.O.C.)
{yangsyu, cmwang}@iis.sinica.edu.tw
a29066049@gmail.com

Abstract. Quality of service (QoS) is a critical nonfunctional property and a criterion for the selection of web services (WSs); due to its importance, many QoS-aware or QoS-based approaches have been proposed and developed. However, with the existence of numerous approach-based studies of QoS of WSs, we consider that the deficiency in the existing research is the lack of a systematic investigation and analysis of real-world QoS data to discover and understand the characteristics of such data. Therefore, in this paper, we first define a number of research questions related to the properties of WSs' QoS that could be interesting to WS/QoS researchers. Then, two real-world, large-scale QoS datasets are chosen, and a number of experiments that address the defined research questions are designed and performed on those datasets. Finally, based on the experimental results, the answer to each research question is discussed in detail.

The main contribution of this paper is to empirically reveal and confirm several useful and interesting properties of real-world QoS. For example, it is found that the distance between a service consumer and its invoked WS does not influence the invocation failure rates of the WSs; however, this distance is indeed correlated to the consumer-perceived WS performance in that a shorter distance can lead to a shorter response time and higher throughput (i.e., a better performance) of WSs according to our experimental results.

Keywords: Web services · Quality of Service · Empirical study

1 Introduction

To date, most QoS-based research about web services (WSs) has concentrated on technical and approach-based studies, including the invention and development of diverse QoS-based approaches for various purposes and operations. Given these approach-based QoS studies, we consider that a shortcoming of current research is the failure to explore empirically and in depth the real-world QoS values of WSs. In the real world, as demonstrated later in this paper, the actual QoS values of WSs are not static but vary with a number of dynamic QoS factors, such as different service consumers and invocation times. In addition, in many cases, the real QoS values do not match those claimed and published by the providers of WSs [1]. Therefore, under such circumstances, an empirical analysis of characteristics and particular features of real-world QoS observations is necessary and valuable.

© Springer Nature Switzerland AG 2019
J. E. Ferreira et al. (Eds.): SCC 2019, LNCS 11515, pp. 48–65, 2019.
https://doi.org/10.1007/978-3-030-23554-3_4

In this paper, we perform an empirical analysis of two large-scale, real-world QoS datasets to obtain some useful observations and insights. First, to be specific and clear regarding the issues studied in this work, we explicitly define the QoS-related research questions (RQs) investigated and answered in this paper, including the motivation for the definition and study of each RQ. Then, to answer the defined RQs, a set of empirical experiments and a number of QoS datasets for the performance of those experiments are needed. In this study, two complementary QoS datasets − consumer-aware and time-aware dynamic QoS datasets − are selected and used in our experiments; these datasets are chosen to represent the phenomenon that, when using the same WS, the experienced QoS values vary with the service consumer and invocation time. Using these two QoS datasets, we design and perform a number of experiments for each RQ, and then the results of all experiments are described and discussed in detail to determine the answer to each RQ.

Below, the contributions of this paper are briefly described. First, we present an empirical study of real-world dynamic QoS observations, which is rarely seen in the current QoS research of WSs. Second, our answers to the RQs and the observations and insights obtained from investigating real-world QoS observations could be valuable and relevant to both service consumers and QoS/WS researchers. For example, our experimental results show that the response times of WS invocations increase with the larger geographical distance between a service consumer and the invoked WS; based on this finding, service consumers are recommended to use WSs located as close as possible. As for the researchers, the relationship between the QoS correlations of two service consumers/WSs and their distances is empirically confirmed in this study.

The remainder of this paper is organized as follows. First, Sect. 2 defines our QoS-related research questions, including the motivation for each. Then, Sect. 3 introduces the two dynamic QoS datasets used in our experiments and describes the design of the experiments for each studied RQ. Subsequently, the experimental results are demonstrated in Sect. 4, and they are discussed in detail in Sect. 5 to obtain the answers to our research questions. Finally, Sect. 6 concludes this paper and describes directions of our future work.

2 Research Questions

This section explicitly defines the QoS-related research questions studied in this paper. In addition, we describe the motivations for the study of the defined RQs and how the answers to the RQs could be useful and helpful to WS stakeholders (i.e., service consumers and providers).

RQ1. What are the geographic distributions of real-world WSs and their consumers?

At present, most public and business WSs are globally accessible through the Internet without any geographic restrictions, and their geographic locations are rarely considered by their consumers and researchers because when discovering and using services, in most cases, the functional and nonfunctional properties of WSs, rather than the locations of the WSs, are the main consideration. Thus, this RQ fills the gap in the research of the geographic distribution of real-world WSs and their consumers.

Furthermore, in addition to understanding the geographic locations of WSs and their consumers, the answer to this RQ is also used in other QoS-related RQs as the criterion for their statistics. For example, when studying RQ3 defined below, an analysis of reliability/availability of WSs in terms of the country (location) of WSs is performed. Note that this RQ is in fact unrelated to QoS.

RQ2. What are the distances between the stakeholders of WSs?
This is this paper's other RQ that is unrelated to QoS, and as in the case of RQ1, the answer to this RQ is also used in the experiments for the following QoS-related RQs as the criterion for their statistics. In practice, when selecting services, most service consumers do not consider the distances between them and the WSs they invoke; thus, to the best of our knowledge, this topic is also rarely considered by either academia or industry. However, as demonstrated later in our analysis, in fact, the distance between a WS and its consumers indeed significantly affects the QoS of the WS experienced by the service consumers; thus, it is meaningful and helpful to investigate this RQ. Moreover, in this RQ, the distances between different WSs and disparate service consumers are also considered to validate the fundamental assumption of some location-aware QoS approaches (e.g., the authors of [2] state that closer service consumers/WSs experience more similar QoS due to their common or similar network environments and infrastructure).

RQ3. What is the reliability/availability of real-world WSs?
One of the most critical nonfunctional properties and considerations for the clients and end-users of diverse software systems, is the systems' reliability and availability; in general, the temporal availability of business systems must be higher than 99.99% (i.e., such systems must be accessible at least 99.99% of time during one year). WSs are external software components developed to serve consumers that offer diverse functionalities and benefits over the Internet, and they are mostly owned and run by outside companies. Because the use of WSs involves many uncertainties (e.g., Internet connectivity problems and nonfunctional WS servers), the reliability and availability of real-world WSs are a critical concern that merits a detailed investigation based on the real-world availability and reliability data of WSs.

RQ4. What is the performance of real-world WSs?
Currently, many systems and applications rely heavily on external WSs to function normally; therefore, the performance aspects of WSs, such as their response times and throughputs, have been an issue of concern in both research and industry. In addition to devising diverse approaches to accommodate the variable performance of WSs, observing and analyzing real-world QoS data of WSs and how they vary with different factors may be particularly critical and useful. As mentioned, WSs are mostly owned by others, and thus, it is difficult for outside parties to improve the performance of WSs that are affected by internal factors. Nevertheless, one way this can be accomplished by service consumers is by determining the best practices of using WSs by studying the historical performance of WSs. For example, it might theoretically be possible to obtain shorter response times (better performance) of WSs by using services located in closer areas or in different time zones to avoid peak-time workloads and heavy network traffic.

RQ5. What are the correlations between QoS observations?
This RQ would be interesting and helpful to WS/QoS researchers, especially those who try to devise approaches to estimate and predict QoS values. In QoS forecasting research, to obtain accurate prediction results, many approaches are based on the assumption that there are positive correlations between QoS values of different service consumers/WSs, and it is possible to enhance prediction performance by considering these positive QoS correlations. For example, the authors of [3] observe the existence of positive correlations between time series of disparate QoS attributes of a WS, and propose a multivariate time series approach using both the historical QoS time series data and the positive QoS correlations between attributes to accurately estimate future QoS values. As another example, service recommendation approaches based on collaborative filtering (CF), such as [4], use QoS correlations to identify similar service consumers and services (providers) so that the unknown QoS values can be predicted based on the QoS information from these similar consumers and services. However, although QoS correlations have been widely used in QoS research, no large-scale, systematic studies confirming the existence, generality and strength of QoS correlations exist.

3   QoS Datasets and Design of Experiments

This section first introduces and discusses two real-world, large-scale QoS datasets selected and studied in this work; then, we describe in detail the design of the experiments on the two targeted QoS datasets used to obtain the answers to the defined RQs.

3.1   QoS Datasets and Basic Statistics

Below, we first introduce the criteria of our QoS dataset selection process. A number of public QoS datasets for WSs are available to researchers, and these datasets have been widely used in diverse QoS-based studies to evaluate and validate the proposed QoS-aware approaches. However, a common problem in many of existing datasets is the insufficient number of WSs for which the QoS values have been collected and recorded. For example, the QoS dataset provided by the authors of [5] has been widely used in time series-based QoS forecasting research, such as [6, 7]; however, a deficiency in this dataset is that only the QoS values of 10 real-world WSs have been sampled and recorded. In this paper, for generality and reliability of our answers to the defined RQs, two large-scale QoS datasets containing QoS values gathered from a large number of WSs are used. In other words, the main criterion for the selection of QoS datasets is their number of sampled WSs. In the two selected QoS datasets, the counts of included WSs are 5825 and 807, respectively. Furthermore, another criterion in the selection of QoS datasets is the availability of location data for the sampled service consumers and WSs. In our study and experiments, the locations of service consumers and WSs are essential, especially for studies of RQ1 and RQ2. Although many QoS datasets are currently available, most of them contain only QoS values without any location data. In the two selected QoS data sources, however, both IP addresses and geographic locations (longitudes and latitudes) of service consumers and WSs are available. Finally, the main causes of the changes in QoS values in each of the two QoS data sources are different, leading to diversity in the dynamic factors that cause QoS variations. As to dynamic QoS attributes, two general factors of changing QoS values have been identified [1] thus far, namely, different service consumers and disparate invocation times. In this study, both of these factors are considered by performing experiments on a consumer-aware QoS dataset and a time-aware QoS dataset.

Below, the two selected QoS datasets are first described in detail; then, their basic statistics are presented. The first adopted QoS dataset is *dataset1* of the well-known *WSDREAM* project [8], which contains QoS values for two different QoS attributes, namely, response times and throughputs. More specifically, the dataset in fact comprises two QoS matrices; the first matrix represents the collected response time data, and the second matrix contains the recorded throughput values. The dimensionality of both QoS matrices is two; the first dimension represents different service consumers, and the second dimension identifies disparate real-world WSs. In other words, each entry in the two matrices represents the real value of a dynamic QoS attribute experienced by a service consumer invoking a WS. This QoS dataset, due to the variations in a WS's QoS values caused by the different WS invocations made by disparate service consumers, is considered a *consumer-aware* QoS dataset. Another QoS dataset considered in this study was collected and provided by the authors of [9] and contains only response time data. This response time dataset can also be viewed as a two-dimensional QoS matrix; however, the first dimension in this matrix represents different WS invocation times, and the other dimension still represents the different WSs. In this dataset, only the response times of the same service consumer invoking disparate WSs were sampled and recorded. For the invocations of the same WS, the reason for the varying QoS values in this dataset is the difference in timing of invocations, and thus, this dataset is considered a *time-aware* QoS dataset.

Below, Tables 1 and 2 present the basic properties of the first selected QoS dataset, and Tables 3 and 4 do so for the second dataset. The properties pertaining to the number of service consumers and WSs contained in the first dataset are described in Table 1. Note that in *dataset1* of the WSDREAM project, not all of the locations of WSs are available. In Table 2, the statistics of the two QoS matrices contained in *dataset1* of WSDREAM are shown. In these two QoS matrices, some QoS values are invalid and unrecorded. More specifically, if the WS invocation made by a service consumer to a WS had failed, the corresponding QoS value was set to zero to indicate the failure. Table 3 presents the properties of the two dimensions of the QoS dataset provided by the authors of [9] and the statistics of the QoS values in this dataset. The statistics of QoS time series of this time-aware QoS dataset (namely, the four basic statistical properties of the means and standard deviations of the QoS time series contained in the dataset) are described in Table 4. In Table 3, the statistical results are based on viewing each entry in the QoS matrix as an independent value. However, in this time-aware QoS dataset, the entries in the same column in fact belong to the same QoS time series; thus, we also perform some basic statistical calculations for the QoS time series contained in this dataset.

3.2   Design of Experiments

In this section, we elaborate on the design of our experiments used to answer the defined research questions.

Table 1. Properties of the two dimensions of *dataset1* of the *WSDREAM* project.

	dataset1 of WSDREAM (consumer-aware)
Number of service consumers	339 (valid location information is available for all)
Number of WSs	5825 (valid location information is only provided for 5004 WSs)
Number of service consumers' countries	31
Number of WSs' countries	74
Number of entries	1974675 (339 by 5825)

Table 2. Statistics of the QoS values contained in *dataset1* of the *WSDREAM* project.

	Response time matrix	Throughput matrix
Number of valid entries	1873838 (94.89%)	1831253 (92.73%)
Mean	0.9085	47.5616
Median	0.32	13.953
Standard deviation	1.9726	110.7971
Minimum	0.001	0.004
Maximum	19.999	1000

Table 3. Properties of the two dimensions (invocation times and web services) of the QoS dataset provided by the authors of [9] and the statistics of the QoS values of the dataset.

	QoS dataset of [9] (time-aware)
Number of invocation times	100
Number of WSs	807 (valid location information is only provided for 405 WSs)
Number of WSs' countries	20
Mean	0.7457
Median	0.453
Standard deviation	1853
Minimum	0.015
Maximum	53.095

RQ1. In both of the considered QoS datasets, the IP addresses and geographic locations (latitudes and longitudes) of their service consumers and WSs are available. Therefore, to determine and analyze geographic distributions, we count the numbers of service consumers and WSs in each country that appears in the dataset. Note that the total numbers of countries in both QoS datasets have already been stated in Tables 1 and 3; thus, here we focus on how many service consumers/WSs are within each country.

RQ2. In both of the considered QoS datasets, the latitudes and longitudes of service consumers and WSs are available. Accordingly, we calculate and analyze both the

Table 4. Statistics (means and standard deviations) of the QoS time series contained in the dataset provided by the authors of [9].

Average of the means of RT TSs	0.7457
Median of the means of RT TSs	0.521
Minimum of the means of RT TSs	0.0272
Maximum of the means of RT TSs	34.504
Average of the SDs of RT TSs	0.289
Median of the SDs of RT TSs	0.18
Minimum of the SDs of RT TSs	0.008
Maximum of the SDs of RT TSs	4.779

geographic distances and time zone differences between service consumers and WSs, between two service consumers, and between two WSs. Moreover, due to the large number of pairs, the overall results are calculated and illustrated in forms of percentiles. More specifically, we demonstrate the statistics of the geographic distances and time zone differences using 1%, 20%, 40%, 60%, 80%, and 100% percentiles. As a result, the overall distributions of data can be clearly observed.

RQ3. To study the reliability of real-world WSs, we rely on the QoS observations provided by the first QoS dataset, and, similarly to [10], base our calculations and analysis on the probability of WS invocation failures. As to the second QoS dataset, there is no data that can indicate the reliability of WSs it contains.

For both QoS matrices, we calculate their invocation failure rates in terms of three different criteria, namely, the countries where service consumers and WSs are located, the consumer-service geographic distance, and the consumer-service time zone difference. For the first criterion, there are four different results, namely, the outcomes from the four different combinations of countries of service consumers/WSs and the two types of QoS attributes. Then, the study based on the last two criteria considers the relationships between the WS invocation failures and the geographic distances and time zone differences. Note that the calculations for these two criteria rely on the answer to RQ2 and require that we compute the WS invocation failure rates for each geographic distance and time zone difference percentile region.

RQ4. To study RQ4, the two QoS datasets and two length-based criteria are considered. For the two consumer-aware QoS matrices, we calculate their average QoS values (response time and throughput) for each geographic distance/time zone difference percentile region. As for the time-aware QoS matrix, because it consists of response time QoS time series, we focus on the means and standard deviations of these QoS time series. The means of QoS time series are used to assess the performance of invoked WSs, and their standard deviations can be used to observe the stability of WSs' performance.

RQ5. For the calculation of correlations between QoS observations, in this paper, we adopt the widely used Pearson correlation coefficient (PCC) due to its superior accuracy and advantages over other methods [11]. First, in the two consumer-aware QoS matrices, we consider the QoS observations of a service consumer gathered from invoking different WSs and the QoS observations of a WS obtained from its different service consumers as the feature vectors of the service consumer and of the WS, respectively. Then, for pairs of service consumers and pairs of WSs, we compute their PCC-based correlations based on their QoS feature vectors. Finally, to observe the relationships between the consumer-consumer/WS-WS correlations and the geographic distances/time zone differences, similar to the experiments for RQ4, we also calculate the average correlation value for each geographic distance/time zone difference percentile region. In addition, based on the two consumer-aware QoS matrices, we also compute the correlations between these two matrices (i.e., the correlations between two disparate QoS attributes). In summary, in these experiments, we systematically study and examine the correlations between two service consumers, between two WSs, and between two different QoS attributes. As for the time-aware QoS dataset, the PCC correlations between the two QoS time series in this matrix are calculated and considered (i.e., each QoS time series is viewed as a feature vector, and then the PCC values are computed for each combination of two feature vectors).

4 Analytic Results

This section illustrates the results of our experiments. Figures 1, 2 and Table 5 show the results used to answer RQ1, while Tables 6, 7, 8, 9 and 10 pertain to RQ2. The results of the experiments relevant to RQ3 are shown in Table 11 and Fig. 3. Finally, Figs. 4 and 5 demonstrate the experimental results of RQ4, while Figs. 6, 7 and 8 pertain to RQ5.

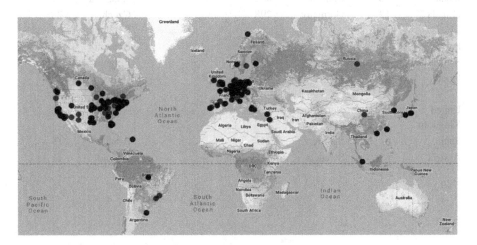

Fig. 1. Geographic distribution of service consumers in *dataset1* of WSDREAM.

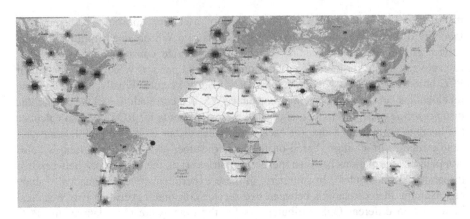

Fig. 2. Geographic distribution of WSs in *dataset1* of WSDREAM.

Table 5. Distributions by country of service consumers and WSs in the two considered QoS datasets (Top 10 countries).

dataset1 of WSDREAM				QoS dataset of [9]			
Service consumers		WSs		Service consumers		WSs	
Country	Number	Country	Number	Country	Number	Country	Number
United States	161	United States	2395	Australia	1	China	137
Germany	41	United Kingdom	510			Canada	57
Japan	16	Canada	432			Australia	39
Canada	12	Germany	298			Czech Republic	23
Poland	12	China	271			Denmark	22
Switzerland	9	Italy	221			Belgium	21
France	9	France	202			United States	19
United Kingdom	8	Netherlands	116			Austria	18
Spain	6	Spain	94			Brazil	17
Austria	6	Sweden	87			Iceland	11

Table 6. Various percentiles of consumer-WS distance distribution in *dataset1* of *WSDREAM*.

Service consumer-WS distance distribution		
Percentile	Geographic distance (km)	Time zone difference
1%	128	0
20%	1459	1
40%	4031	3
60%	7484	6
80%	9131	9
100%	19853	19

Table 7. Various percentiles of consumer-consumer distance distribution in *dataset1* of *WSDREAM*.

Consumer-consumer distance distribution		
Percentile	Geographic distance (km)	Time zone difference
1%	50	0
20%	1401	1
40%	4184	3
60%	7558	6
80%	9272	9
100%	19601	16

Table 8. Various percentiles of WS-WS distance distribution in *dataset1* of WSDREAM.

WS-WS distance distribution		
Percentile	Geographic distance (km)	Time zone difference
1%	0	0
20%	1502	1
40%	3894	3
60%	7327	6
80%	8972	9
100%	19958	22

Table 9. Various percentiles of consumer-WS distance distribution in the time-aware QoS dataset provided by [9].

Service consumer-WS distance distribution		
Percentile	Geographic distance (km)	Time zone difference
1%	33	0
20%	8230	2
40%	9122	2
60%	14884	8
80%	16265	14
100%	17681	17

Table 10. Various percentiles of WS-WS distance distribution in the time-aware QoS dataset provided by [9].

WS-WS distance distribution		
Percentile	Geographic distance (km)	Time zone difference
1%	0	0
20%	1984	1
40%	7491	6
60%	8779	6
80%	11693	12
100%	19902	17

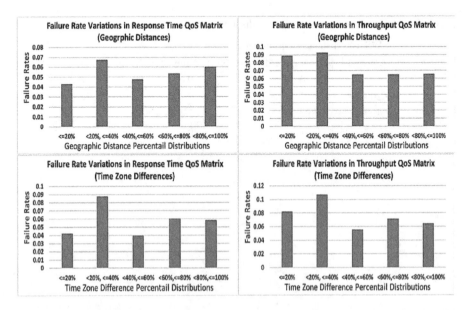

Fig. 3. Invocation failure rates for various geographic distance/time zone difference percentiles in *dataset1* of WSDREAM.

Table 11. Service consumer and WS invocation failure rates by country in *dataset1* of WSDREAM (Top 10 worst countries).

Response time matrix				Throughput matrix			
Serv. consumers		WSs		Serv. consumers		WSs	
Country	Rate	Country	Rate	Country	Rate	Country	Rate
China	.103*	India	.454	Austria	.106	Bahamas	1*
Austria	.078	Colombia	.334	China	.089*	India	.437
United States	.056	Egypt	.268*	Italy	.08	Colombia	.334
Japan	.054	Thailand	.196	Ireland	.08	Egypt	.268*
Korea	.053	France	.133	Hungary	.078	France	.138
Russia	.051*	Vietnam	.13	United States	.078	Thailand	.137
Spain	.05	Greece	.109	United Kingdom	.077	Greece	.109
Israel	.05	Kazakhstan	0.097*	Poland	.075	Serbia and Montenegro	.109
Italy	.05	Malaysia	.093	Sweden	.073*	Japan	.103
Cyprus	.049	Canada	.082	Slovenia	.073*	Germany	.097

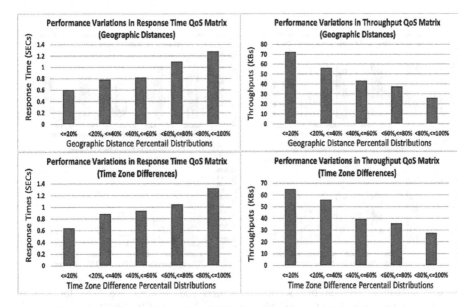

Fig. 4. Performance (response time and throughput) for various geographic distance/time zone difference percentiles in *dataset1* of WSDREAM.

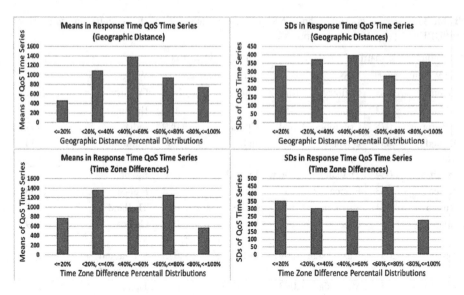

Fig. 5. Means and standard deviations of QoS time series for various geographic distance/time zone difference percentiles in the time-aware QoS dataset provided by [9].

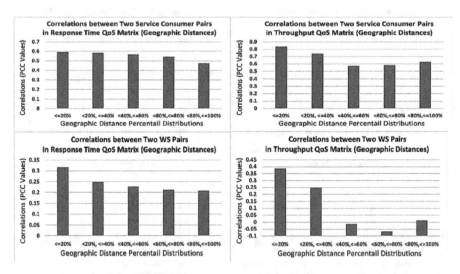

Fig. 6. Correlations between two service consumers and between two WSs for various percentiles of the distribution of geographic distance in *dataset1* of WSDREAM.

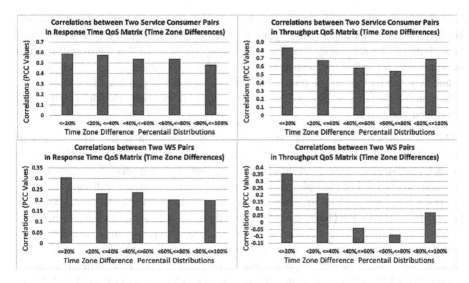

Fig. 7. Correlations between two service consumers and between two WSs for various percentiles of the distribution of time zone difference in *dataset1* of WSDREAM.

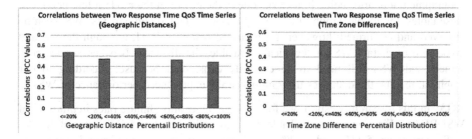

Fig. 8. Correlations between two WSs for various percentiles of the distributions of geographic distance and time zone difference in the time-aware QoS dataset provided by [9].

5 Discussion

In this section, we consecutively discuss the answers to the research questions defined in Sect. 2 based on the experimental results demonstrated in Sect. 4.

RQ1. First, according to the statistical data shown in Table 1, the service consumers and WSs in *dataset1* of *WSDREAM* are scattered around the world in 31 and 74 different countries, respectively. As to the second QoS dataset, the WSs are located in 20 different countries according to Table 3. Furthermore, from Figs. 1 and 2 that show the geographic distributions of the service consumers and WSs in *dataset1* of *WSDREAM*, it can be observed that most service consumers and WSs recorded in the dataset are located in the U.S. and Europe; their detailed numbers are shown in Table 5. According to the left part of Table 5, most service consumers and WSs in *dataset1* of

WSDREAM are in the U.S. (and more broadly, in the North America and Europe); however, in the other dataset (the right part of Table 5), it is China that hosts the most WSs, followed by the North America and Europe. We observe that the overall trend in these datasets regarding the hosting and use of WSs is that most service consumers are in and WSs are located in and owned by entities in the developed countries, which may reflect the difference in the extent of digitalization between the developing and developed countries.

RQ2. In Tables 6, 7, 8, 9 and 10, a common phenomenon is the wide ranges of geographic distances and time zone differences between two service-oriented instances (namely, between a service consumer and a WS, between two service consumers, and between two WSs). For example, as shown in Table 6, the geographic distance between a service consumer and its invoked WS in the first dataset varies from 128 km (1% percentile) to 19853 km (100% percentile, i.e., the longest geographic distance between a service consumer and its invoked WS in the dataset), while the time zone difference ranges from being in the same time zone (i.e., zero difference) to 19 time zones. We consider these wide ranges of geographic distances and time zone differences to be reasonable; additionally, they match the graphical results shown in Figs. 1 and 2, and the detailed numerical distributions described in Table 5 in that both real-world service consumers and WSs are scattered in various places around the world, and successful WS invocations can involve service consumers and WSs located in different regions, with geographic boundaries being immaterial due to the power of the modern Internet. From these tables, the globalization of the use of service-oriented components (WSs) can be observed and confirmed; however, as discussed below in RQ4, although the use and invocation of distant WSs is technically feasible, the distances between service consumers and WSs still need to be carefully considered because, according to our empirical results, the distances truly influence the experienced performance of WSs.

RQ3. In this research question, we focus on the invocation failure rates in *dataset1* of WSDREAM. First, according to Table 2, the overall invocation failure rates of the two QoS matrices are 5.11% and 7.27%, which are definitely not good enough, especially for commercial business systems. This empirical result may indicate a downside and a risk of using WSs that are mostly external components, the invoking of which thus potentially involves many uncertain factors (e.g., disconnected networks or heavily loaded WS servers). Therefore, when using WSs, some mechanisms for tolerating, preventing, or correcting failures, such as service level agreement (SLA)-aware runtime service selection and dynamic binding approaches, must be integrated and used together with the invoked WSs to ensure the satisfactory availability and reliability of the developed service-oriented systems.

Considering the invocation failure rates in different countries (i.e., the results listed in Table 11), the results are even worse in the top 10 worst countries. For example, in the right part of Table 11, which demonstrates the invocation failure rates of service consumers and WSs for the top 10 worst countries in the throughput QoS matrix of *dataset1* of WSDREAM, the rates are from 7.5% to 10% for service consumers in these countries and from 10% to 100% for WSs. Note that the data in Table 11 marked with an asterisk (*) indicates that the number of samples (service consumers or WSs) is only one. These inferior results further emphasize the need for an effective invocation failure resolution infrastructure for (or an approach to) the use of WSs.

The relationship between the invocation failure rate and the geographic distance/time zone difference is illustrated by the four bar charts shown in Fig. 3. In the figure, a common trend of the data is that the failure rate initially increases with the longer distance (i.e., the first two bars in each bar chart); however, the rate declines substantially at the third bar in each chart (i.e., the data between 40% and 60% percentiles), and finally a rising curve is observed in each chart during the last three percentile regions (between 40% and 100% percentiles). Overall, these statistical results seem to show that no permanent positive correlation between the invocation failure rate and the distance between a service consumer and the invoked WS can be observed. In other words, when selecting a service, the shorter distance between a service consumer and a WS did not guarantee a relatively lower invocation failure rate. However, although the distance did not affect the invocation failure rate, geographic distances in fact influence the consumer-perceived performance of WSs, as discussed in the next research question.

RQ4. Tables 2 and 4 show that the performance of WSs, including their response times and throughputs, can vary substantially. For example, in Table 2, the response times of WSs change from 0.001 s (i.e., the minimum in the response time QoS matrix of *dataset1* of WSDREAM) to 19.99 s (the maximum). Thus, due to this very large performance variation, it is critical to identify the factors that influence the performance of WSs the most, so that the identified factors can be controlled or optimized during or before the use of WSs.

Based on the results shown in Figs. 4 and 5, in this paper, we consider that one of the main factors that significantly influences the consumer-perceived performance of WSs is the distance (including both geographic distance and time zone difference) between a service consumer and the invoked WS. More specifically, for example, a clear trend observed in the four bar charts of Fig. 4 is that if the distance between a service consumer and the invoked WS increases, both the experienced response times and throughput values degrade accordingly (i.e., longer response times and lower throughput values are observed). Thus, in this scenario, a reasonable suggestion is to select WSs that are as close as possible to service consumers.

On the other hand, in the left part of Fig. 5, which illustrates the mean values of the response time QoS time series provided in [9], the relationship between the mean response time of the WSs and the distance between a service consumer and a WS is not always characterized by a positive correlation. Given the empirical data shown in the left part of Fig. 5, however, we still regard choosing to use a closer WS as a better strategy for obtaining a higher probability of a relatively better QoS performance of WSs because the mean response times of WSs included in the first bar (i.e., the data below 20% percentile) are still smaller than the others in most cases.

RQ5. In both Figs. 6 and 7, considering the correlations between QoS feature vectors of two service consumers and between those of two WSs, it is observed that the PCC values for pairs of service-oriented instances (i.e., two service consumers or two WSs) decrease as the distance between two instances increases. Thus, this empirical result may support the approach used by some QoS-based studies, such as [12], to improve performance by selecting and using the QoS information obtained from geographically closer service consumers/WSs. In addition, although a reversed and rising trend of correlation values can be observed in 60% to 100% percentile regions in some bar charts of Figs. 6 and 7, these correlation values changing in the reverse and upward direction are still lower than the corresponding correlation values observed in the initial percentile region (i.e., the values represented by the first bar in each bar chart). Thus, it is still suggested to preferentially consider the QoS information for closer service-oriented instances.

According to Figs. 6 and 7, another useful observation is that the correlations between two service consumers (e.g., in the left part of Fig. 6, based on the response time data, the PCC values for correlations between two service consumers are between 0.47 and 0.59) are higher than the correlations between two WSs (the response time-based PCC values for correlations between two WSs are between 0.2 and 0.31) in both QoS matrices of *dataset1* of *WSDREAM*. Given this observation, it is suggested to preferentially rely on user-based QoS information (i.e., the QoS data obtained from a set of similar service consumers) when using neighborhood-based collaborative filtering (CF) approaches, such as [11], to obtain the estimates and predictions of unknown QoS values.

6   Conclusions

Numerous QoS-based or QoS-aware approaches have been considered in existing studies; however, empirical and systematic investigations of real-world QoS values themselves remain rare. Thus, in this paper, we first define five QoS-related research questions, and then select two large-scale, real-world QoS datasets as the basis of our study. To answer the defined research questions, several experiments on the selected QoS datasets are designed and performed. Finally, the answers to the research questions are discussed in detail based on the empirical experimental results.

In this paper, overall, we make a number of valuable and useful observations regarding the QoS of web services. First, it is observed that both service consumers and WSs are globally distributed, and thus, the distances between them can vary substantially, which influences the perceived performance of WS invocations and the correlations between two service consumers/WSs. We also observe that the invocation failure rates of WSs are not always positively correlated to the distance between a service consumer and the invoked WS; however, this factor of distance truly affects the performance of WSs in that shorter distances can lead to better performance. Finally, another major QoS property affected by distance is the correlation between the QoS features of two service consumers/WSs; similar to WS performance, shorter distances can also result in higher correlations. These empirical findings could be helpful for the design of QoS-aware or QoS-based approaches and the use of real-world WSs.

In the future, we plan to search for and obtain more large-scale, real-world QoS datasets to collect more QoS samples to perform QoS studies onto enhance the generality and persuasiveness of our experimental results and the corresponding discussion. Additionally, given a large number of QoS datasets, for each defined research question, we try to formally define a set of common patterns of experiments (i.e., computational processes and algorithms) that can be generally performed on different QoS datasets to obtain the required experimental (statistical) results for subsequent analysis. Finally, we also plan to use the network distance measurement technology to replace the geographic distances used in this study to obtain the precise distance between two service-oriented instances.

References

1. Fanjiang, Y.-Y., Syu, Y., Kuo, J.-Y.: Search based approach to forecasting QoS attributes of web services using genetic programming. Inf. Softw. Technol. **80**, 158–174 (2016)
2. Hu, Y., Peng, Q., Hu, X., Yang, R.: Time aware and data sparsity tolerant web service recommendation based on improved collaborative filtering. IEEE Trans. Serv. Comput. **8**(5), 782–794 (2015)
3. Ye, Z., Mistry, S.K., Bouguettaya, A., Dong, H.: Long-term QoS-aware cloud service composition using multivariate time series analysis. IEEE Trans. Serv. Comput. **9**, 382–393 (2014)
4. Zibin, Z., Hao, M., Lyu, M.R., King, I.: Collaborative web service QoS prediction via neighborhood integrated matrix factorization. IEEE Trans. Serv. Comput. **6**(3), 289–299 (2013)
5. Cavallo, B., Penta, M.D., Canfora, G.: An empirical comparison of methods to support QoS-aware service selection, presented at the Proceedings of the 2nd International Workshop on Principles of Engineering Service-Oriented Systems, Cape Town, South Africa (2010)
6. Syu, Y., Kuo, J.-Y., Fanjiang, Y.-Y.: Time series forecasting for dynamic quality of web services: an empirical study. J. Syst. Softw. **134**, 279–303 (2017)
7. Amin, A., Colman, A., Grunske, L.: An approach to forecasting QoS attributes of web services based on ARIMA and GARCH models. In: 2012 IEEE 19th International Conference on Web Services (ICWS), pp. 74–81 (2012)
8. Zheng, Z., Zhang, Y., Lyu, M.: Investigating QoS of real-world web services. IEEE Trans. Serv. Comput. **7**, 32–39 (2012)
9. Amin, A., Grunske, L., Colman, A.: An automated approach to forecasting QoS attributes based on linear and non-linear time series modeling, presented at the Proceedings of the 27th IEEE/ACM International Conference on Automated Software Engineering, Essen, Germany (2012)
10. Zheng, Z., Lyu, M.R.: Personalized reliability prediction of web services. ACM Trans. Softw. Eng. Methodol. **22**(2), 1–25 (2013)
11. Zibin, Z., Hao, M., Lyu, M.R., King, I.: QoS-aware web service recommendation by collaborative filtering. IEEE Trans. Serv. Comput. **4**(2), 140–152 (2011)
12. Wang, X., Zhu, J., Zheng, Z., Song, W., Shen, Y., Lyu, M.R.: A spatial-temporal QoS prediction approach for time-aware web service recommendation. ACM Trans. Web **10**(1), 1–25 (2016)

Towards the Readiness of Learning Analytics Data for Micro Learning

Jiayin Lin[1]($\boxtimes$), Geng Sun[1]($\boxtimes$), Jun Shen[1,2]($\boxtimes$), Tingru Cui[1]($\boxtimes$),
Ping Yu[1]($\boxtimes$), Dongming Xu[3]($\boxtimes$), Li Li[4]($\boxtimes$),
and Ghassan Beydoun[5]($\boxtimes$)

[1] School of Computing and Information Technology, University of Wollongong,
Wollongong, Australia
jl461@uowmail.edu.au, {Gsun,Jshen,
tingru,ping}@uow.edu.au
[2] Research Lab of Electronics, Department of EE and CS,
Massachusetts Institute of Technology, Cambridge, USA
[3] UQ Business School, The University of Queensland, Brisbane, Australia
d.xu@business.uq.edu.au
[4] Faculty of Computer and Information Science, Southwest University,
Chongqing, China
lily@swu.edu.cn
[5] School of Information System and Modelling,
University of Technology Sydney, Sydney, Australia
ghassan.beydoun@uts.edu.au

Abstract. With the development of data mining and machine learning techniques, data-driven based technology-enhanced learning (TEL) has drawn wider attention. Researchers aim to use established or novel computational methods to solve educational problems in the 'big data' era. However, the readiness of data appears to be the bottleneck of the TEL development and very little research focuses on investigating the data scarcity and inappropriateness in the TEL research. This paper is investigating an emerging research topic in the TEL domain, namely micro learning. Micro learning consists of various technical themes that have been widely studied in the TEL research field. In this paper, we firstly propose a micro learning system, which includes recommendation, segmentation, annotation, and several learning-related prediction and analysis modules. For each module of the system, this paper reviews representative literature and discusses the data sources used in these studies to pinpoint their current problems and shortcomings, which might be debacles for more effective research outcomes. Accordingly, the data requirements and challenges for learning analytics in micro learning are also investigated. From a research contribution perspective, this paper serves as a basis to depict and understand the current status of the readiness of data sources for the research of micro learning.

Keywords: Micro learning · Learning analytics · Machine learning ·
Data mining · Data insufficiency

© Springer Nature Switzerland AG 2019
J. E. Ferreira et al. (Eds.): SCC 2019, LNCS 11515, pp. 66–76, 2019.
https://doi.org/10.1007/978-3-030-23554-3_5

1 Introduction

The rapid evolution of technologies and the changes in people's lifestyle make technology-enhanced learning (TEL) become a hot topic in recent years. In the context of big data, despite the technical difficulties, data problem is an obvious obstacle for the development of TEL research. As most models are driven by data, sufficient, consistent and complete data is the fundamental factor for system design, model construction, and evaluation for learning analytics. Learning analytics (LA) conventionally involves the evaluation, collection, analysis and reporting of data about learners and their contexts, for the purpose of understanding and optimising learning and environments which it occurs [1]; LA becomes increasingly important when the hype of big data and artificial intelligence are more and more distilled into the education sector.

Among research topics in the TEL area, a notable term, micro learning, represents a novel educational service, which provides users with small chunks of personalized learning materials [2]. Such service aims to enable learning activities being carried out by effectively making use of users' fragmented time, and this service can be applied to different online learning platforms such as traditional learning management system (LMS) and MOOC. We refer to the whole integrated processing flow of a micro learning service as a micro learning system. Micro learning is a representative inter-disciplinary research topic, which is promoted by data mining and machine learning and consists of various technical topics such as recommendation, resource fragmentation, content analysis, and prediction.

In this paper, we focus on discussing the vital application stages that involve LA, and the data requirements and challenges for micro learning. It should be clarified that the strict definition of LA is beyond the scope of this paper. As this paper particularly reviews a portion of representative prior studies, we have left the systematic literature review of the data requirements and challenges as an opportunity for expanded future work. The remainder of this paper is organized as follow. In Sect. 2, before discussing the details of the data sources that used in each processing stage or various LA tasks, we first describe the structure and the key components of our proposed micro learning system. We discuss several representative segmentation and annotation studies and the data sources used in literature in Sect. 3. The data sources used in the recommendation, prediction, and analysis tasks are discussed in Sects. 4 and 5. In Sect. 6, we summarize the data requirements and challenges for the micro learning research. This paper is concluded in Sect. 7.

2 Micro Learning System

As aforementioned, the provision of micro learning is an online educational service, which aims to utilize users' fragmented spare time and offer users small pieces of personalized learning materials. To realize this online service, the system requires several components for learning material preparation and personalized decision-making. Based on the service requirements, a micro learning system consists of three core parts (i.e., non-micro learning material segmentation, learning material annotation, and learning material recommendation) and several prediction and analysis modules, which work together to provide a complete personalized online learning service. In this section, before diving into the details of the data readiness of micro learning, we firstly outline the typical structure of a micro learning system and the data flow of this system, as shown in Fig. 1.

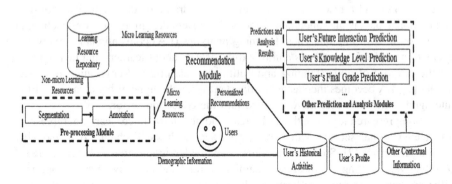

Fig. 1. The structure and the data flow of the proposed micro learning system.

2.1   Pre-processing Model

On many online learning platforms such as LMSs, the duration of consuming a learning material is longer than 15 min [2]. For a micro learning service, non-micro learning materials are logically segmented into coherent knowledge points prior to be delivered to learners. After the segmentation process, an annotation step is required to make learning resources both machine understandable and human understandable, to overcome the lack of interpretability of the micro learning resources. As discussed in many studies [3, 4], proper annotation, indexing, or tagging are essential for the retrieval, recommendation, and reuse of resources.

2.2   Recommendation and Prediction Models

The recommendation phase is central to a micro learning service, which greatly determines what information will be delivered to the users. In the educational domain, as prior studies [5, 6] point out, with the plethora of online learning resources and increasingly frequent formal and informal learning interactions, users can benefit a lot from services which help them quickly and precisely identify the suitable learning resources. Moreover, in the era of big data, more and more learners demand an intelligent system to help them pick suitable information or filter out the irrelevant one [7].

To realize a comprehensive micro learning service, a system should also involve some intelligent prediction and analysis modules to boost decision-making, such as behaviour prediction and performance prediction. With a large number of users, it is impractical to manually analyse each user's learning history or requirements. The prediction and analysis results, such as a user's knowledge level and the difficulty level of learning material, could enrich the information for the system's decision-making processes.

3 Annotation and Segmentation

The task for pre-processing is to transform the non-micro learning materials to the micro learning ones, which consists of segmentation and annotation. Segmentation and annotation are mainly driven by the content information of the learning materials; hence, the readiness of the research data is vital for the research on segmentation and annotation.

As many learning materials are in video format, many studies of annotation and segmentation heavily rely on transforming the image and audio information to textual format [3, 8, 9]. Researchers extract textual metadata by applying Optical Character Recognition (OCR) and Automatic Speech Recognition (ASR) on the lecture videos [8]. The experiment in [8] only involves 20 randomly selected lecture videos from different speakers. The study [3] used natural language processing (NLP) techniques to further mine the extracted textual information in assisting the annotation process. The dataset used in this study was related to Objective Oriented Programming in French, but the details and source of this dataset were not given.

Some segmentation or annotation models are based on the users' demographic information. We refer this demography-based method as the 'crowd-wisdom' method. The log file of users' watching interactions of four edX[1] courses are analysed in the study [10]; the researchers argued that the re-watching peaks of the whole user population might be the crucial knowledge for LA because these peaks of the re-watching point can be used to further identify the boundaries of knowledge points. Another lecture annotation system is proposed in the study [11], but only 21 students were involved. The study [4] proposed a crowd-wisdom based model to integrate annotation results, but only an image dataset [12] was used. A semantic extraction model and a tagging model were proposed in [13] to annotate the online learning resources. However, the data source for model construction and validation was not elaborated in their paper.

4 Recommendation

Recommender system is a hot topic and has been studied for many years, but in the area of micro learning it is still in the embryonic stage. Insufficient, inappropriate and unknown data sources are the main challenges for the research of micro learning recommendation.

4.1 Insufficient Data Source

The term 'insufficient data' means the data used in a study can only partially reflect the underlying issues against the context of potentially bigger data, and the experiment result of recommendation might be biased.

---

[1] https://www.edx.org/.

The study [7] proposed a hybrid recommendation algorithm, which could reflect the timeliness of a learning procedure, but as few as 30 students were involved in this study. Metadata for Architectural Contents in Europe (MACE) and TravelWell datasets were used [14] for training the usage context-boosted recommender system. However, both datasets contain very few users and only a fraction of subjects. One prior study [15] used a convolutional neural network (CNN) to model the latent factors based on the BookCrossing dataset [16]. However, in the e-learning domain, the type of learning materials could be in the format of video, audio, and text, the conventionally trained model was not sophisticated enough for micro learning. The fault tolerance and the capability of self-optimization prompt swarm intelligence and evolutionary computing to be applied in many studies for learning path optimization [17, 18]. However, the sizes of experiments in these study were still defective, as only 80 students were observed [17] and only one chapter of mathematics teaching material was used in [18]. Due to the heterogeneity, insufficient users and/or subjects cannot generally reflect the latent patterns of e-learning scenarios or the whole user population in the real-life micro learning environments.

4.2   Inappropriate and Unknown Data Source

Inappropriate and unknown datasets also impede the development of micro learning. An inappropriate dataset refers to the dataset coming from noisy sources, other domains, or not acquired from a real learning activity; an unknown dataset refers to the one researchers did not mention its source. The experiment results obtained from such dataset could be problematic, unconvincing or unrealistic.

Simulated data was used to construct long short term memory (LSTM) model for learning path recommendation in [19]. However, the authors did not provide any details about the simulation and its validity. The simulated data could be inaccurate, as in most cases the researchers had no prior knowledge about the users or the learning materials, such as users' demographic information. Another prior study [20] used MovieLens [21] dataset to demonstrate that a fuzzy-tree-based collaborative filtering model could boost the recommendation result. However, given MovieLens being not an education-related dataset, using such irrelevant dataset might not truly inspire the problem-solving approach in real recommendation cases in e-learning.

Some studies in recommendation were based on the applications or learning platforms, which had been developed by researchers themselves [7, 22]. For example, in constructing the proposed recommending model, the researchers collected data from an application called 'Itsego' in [22]. Similarly, the study in [7] was based on a learning system developed by researchers themselves. Most of the datasets from self-developed platforms or the LMSs hosted by researchers' affiliations are not open to the public. Prior research [23] demonstrated that an adaptive neuro-fuzzy inference system could recommend users with a suitable format of learning materials. The clustering techniques were used for group recommendation [24]. Nevertheless, both studies did not claim the sources of the datasets they used either. Such non-public datasets or the datasets with unknown sources make these studies difficult to be followed up, imitated, and improved by other research groups.

5 Prediction and Analysis Tasks

The prediction and analysis models are mainly based on the specific user's historical learning activities or the historical activities collected from similar users. Hence, the data requirements of performance prediction and learning analytics is much more rigid than other research topics.

5.1 Learning Performance Prediction

A learner's knowledge level can be modelled by his/her historical performance, and such prediction model can be used to detect struggling learners and assist the systems' decision-making processes. Prior studies [25–27] investigated the relationship between users' behaviour and their quiz scores. These studies aimed to predict the Correct on First Attempt (CFA) of a learner in answering a question. Learner's historical click-stream and grade were used for constructing the model. However, only two courses [28, 29] were studied in [25, 26], while only one course [28] was studied in the paper [27]. Similarly, a study [30] compared various binary classifiers to predict the outcome (fail/pass) of the exam. The dataset used was for the 2016–2017 academic year, recorded by an e-learning platform without mentioning the details of the data source.

5.2 User Behaviour Prediction

User behaviour prediction and analysis are also important for decision-making. As discussed in the study [31], the way how a learner may interact is worthwhile to understand in order to provide fine-grained insights into what particular content may be improved for further modification or adaptation of the learning activities. But only investigating one course [28] is inadequate for training and validating the model proposed in [31]. Another prior study [32] suggested that different watching patterns might represent different cognitive levels, where the users' next behaviours and future performance could be predicted by clicking interactions. However, only one course [33] comprising 48 lecture videos was examined by authors.

6 Data Requirements and Challenges

As discussed in the previous sections, most models involved in the LA systems are data-driven. For a micro learning system, the required data source can be roughly classified into five categories: user' historical learning and interaction records from log files, users' profile and items' content information stored in the relevant databases, and other contextual information captured by the platform and its various plug-ins. The summarization of the utility of the different data types is shown in Table 1.

Table 1. The utility of different types of data

Data type			Utility and description
User-item rating matrix (learning records)			In most cases, users' historical rating is indispensable for constructing a recommender system
Content information	Textual information		Main information sources for segmentation and annotation
	Audio/Video information		
	Other metadata		
User's interaction	Learning interaction	Clickstream	Main information sources for the tasks of performance prediction and analysis. Various prediction and analysis models, such as early prediction and learning path design, are based on the users' interaction records. Demographic information extracted from users' interaction can also be used to improve the recommendation and segmentation results
		Comments	
		User's access log	
	Quiz/Exam performance		
	User's sequential learning history		
User's profile			The main source of the information about user characteristics. Such age and learning interests, which could be used in the user-based collaborative filtering recommender system
Contextual information			For the decision making, contextual information is used as supplementary, which could be time, location, or anything included in the learning activity. It is the key for a context-aware system

6.1 Data Requirement for Recommendation

For a recommender system, users' historical learning activities are indispensable for training and validating the models. In most cases, the information about user's historical activities only exists in the log files and cannot be crawled from online learning platforms or Websites. As discussed in [15], data-driven recommendation methods require extensive historical data, which is difficult to obtain from the e-learning system. A recommending decision should also be made by referencing the contextual information of current learning activity, users' profile, and items' profile. For research purposes, some information components such as the resource descriptions are open to the public and can be crawled from the online learning website. However, some information only exists in the log file or can only be captured via extra plug-ins.

6.2 Data Requirements for Pre-processing

Before the commencement of recommendation, there is a pre-processing stage to get micro learning materials ready and mine the user's relevant information. The segmentation and annotation strategies are mainly based on the content of the learning materials. In addition, some crowd-wisdom based segmentation [10] and annotation [4, 11, 13] models rely on the demographic information about user's historical interactions. Most content information of the learning material is open to the public while the demographic information is not. On the contrary, the vast majority of prediction models and analysis processes are based on the users' historical interaction data such as clickstream, quiz performance and users' comments.

6.3   Current Challenges

Considering the datasets used in the prior studies, except of non-publicity of the dataset, there are three other main obstacles for the research of micro learning, as summarized in Table 2.

Table 2. The problems of used datasets.

Problem of the dataset	Descriptions
Insufficient data [3, 7, 8, 11, 14, 17, 18, 25–27, 32]	Many research teams can only access and use a fraction of learning materials, or only a small number of users or learners are involved in the experiments. Many case studies in this field are based on relatively small samples. For the research in the big data context, the samples involved in the experiments should be able to cover most cases of the real-life application scenarios
Inappropriate data [4, 15, 19, 20]	Due to lack of dataset, some research can only use simulated dataset or the dataset from other domains for experiments. The simulated dataset could be problematic, as in most cases we have very little prior knowledge about the data prior to the experiments or data analysis. Furthermore, the dataset from irrelevant domains could misrepresent the real situation
Unknown data source [3, 7, 13, 22–24]	Many studies do not mention the source or the details of the datasets that they used. A study involving unknown data source make itself impossible to be followed and improved by other researchers, which seriously impedes the development of this research area

Moreover, the datasets from different sources are isolated. This is not brought to sufficient attention from previous studies. Unlike research in some other domains, which often have standard datasets such as ImageNet[2] for object recognition; due to the vague information of learning resources and different curriculum structures, the datasets from different online learning platforms are isolated, making it challenging for next research to reuse the existing data source. For example, the study [8] captured the textual information from video content, and [14] used the co-occurrence information to boost the collaborative filtering result. The textual information is useful in mining semantic information among the learning resources, which may further boost the

---

[2] http://www.image-net.org/.

recommender system as proposed in the study [14]. However, because of the different sources, these two datasets cannot be fused directly.

Although there are initiatives to push a non-profit sharing of research-oriented MOOC data [34], unfortunately, most data from several learning platforms (e.g., edX and Coursera[3]) are still partially open to researchers, or merely open to their partners. Hence, most research teams can but get access to very limited datasets. Researchers demand more complete and diverse data to drive the decision-making system of the online learning service. Hence, effective data fusion is another gap at present and worth for future research.

7 Conclusion and Future Research

In this paper, we discuss and review different datasets used in the representative prior studies on e-learning. For the different processing stage of a micro learning system, the requirements of the data types vary a lot. User's historical rating of learning materials is an essential factor for constructing a recommender system. However, the segmentation and annotation of learning materials rely on the learning content and the demographic information. Other performance prediction and analysis models are primarily based on the user's historical learning records. As discussed above, insufficiency, inappropriateness, and non-publicity of the datasets, as well as the difficulty of data fusion are the main challenges that we are facing and need to deal with.

As most models involved in the proposed system are data-driven, the idea behinds these optimization and analysis strategies have a significant overlap with the other data-driven research topics in the TEL domain. Even though this paper is under the topic of micro learning, many views derived from discussion and analysis of this paper can be extended to other e-learning related research topics. We expect this paper can also support the future research of other TEL related studies. Furthermore, this paper calls for efforts on the construction of effective public datasets for the research of TEL.

Acknowledgement. This research has been carried out with the support of the Australian Research Council Discovery Project, DP180101051, and Natural Science Foundation of China, no. 61877051, and UGPN RCF 2018-2019 project between University of Wollongong and University of Surrey.

References

1. Ferguson, R.: The state of learning analytics in 2012: a review and future challenges. Knowledge Media Institute, Technical report KMI-2012-01 (2012)
2. Sun, G., et al.: MLaaS: a cloud-based system for delivering adaptive micro learning in mobile MOOC learning. IEEE Trans. Serv. Comput. **11**(2), 292–305 (2018)

---

[3] https://www.coursera.org/.

3. Hendez, M., Achour, H.: Keywords extraction for automatic indexing of e-learning resources. In: 2014 World Symposium on Computer Applications & Research (WSCAR). IEEE (2014)
4. Du, X., Zhang, F., Zhang, M., Xu, S., Liu, M.: Research on result integration mechanism based on crowd wisdom to achieve the correlation of resources and knowledge points. In: Wu, T.-T., Huang, Y.-M., Shadieva, R., Lin, L., Starčič, A.I. (eds.) ICITL 2018. LNCS, vol. 11003, pp. 568–577. Springer, Cham (2018). https://doi.org/10.1007/978-3-319-99737-7_60
5. Verbert, K., et al.: Context-aware recommender systems for learning: a survey and future challenges. IEEE Trans. Learn. Technol. 5(4), 318–335 (2012)
6. Manouselis, N., Drachsler, H., Vuorikari, R., Hummel, H., Koper, R.: Recommender systems in technology enhanced learning. In: Ricci, F., Rokach, L., Shapira, B., Kantor, Paul B. (eds.) Recommender Systems Handbook, pp. 387–415. Springer, Boston, MA (2011). https://doi.org/10.1007/978-0-387-85820-3_12
7. Chen, W., et al.: A hybrid recommendation algorithm adapted in e-learning environments. World Wide Web 17(2), 271–284 (2014).
8. Yang, H., Meinel, C.: Content based lecture video retrieval using speech and video text information. IEEE Trans. Learn. Technol. 2, 142–154 (2014)
9. Dessì, D., et al.: Bridging learning analytics and cognitive computing for big data classification in micro-learning video collections. Comput. Hum. Behav. (2018, in Press)
10. Kim, J., et al.: Understanding in-video dropouts and interaction peaks inonline lecture videos. In: Proceedings of the first ACM conference on Learning@ scale conference. ACM (2014)
11. Risko, E.F., et al.: The collaborative lecture annotation system (CLAS): a new TOOL for distributed learning. IEEE Trans. Learn. Technol. 6(1), 4–13 (2013)
12. Welinder, P., et al.: The multidimensional wisdom of crowds. In: Advances in Neural Information Processing Systems (2010)
13. Cernea, D., Del Moral, E., Gayo, J.: SOAF: semantic indexing system based on collaborative tagging. Interdisc. J. E-Learn. Learn. Obj. 4(1), 137–149 (2008)
14. Niemann, K., Wolpers, M.: Usage context-boosted filtering for recommender systems in TEL. In: Hernández-Leo, D., Ley, T., Klamma, R., Harrer, A. (eds.) EC-TEL 2013. LNCS, vol. 8095, pp. 246–259. Springer, Heidelberg (2013). https://doi.org/10.1007/978-3-642-40814-4_20
15. Shu, J., et al.: A content-based recommendation algorithm for learning resources. Multimedia Syst. 24(2), 163–173 (2018)
16. Ziegler, C.-N., et al.: Improving recommendation lists through topic diversification. In: Proceedings of the 14th International Conference on World Wide Web. ACM (2005)
17. Zhao, Q., Zhang, Y., Chen, J.: An improved ant colony optimization algorithm for recommendation of micro-learning path. In: 2016 IEEE International Conference on Computer and Information Technology (CIT). IEEE (2016)
18. Chen, M., et al.: Recommendation of learning path using an improved ACO based on novel coordinate system. In: 2017 6th IIAI International Congress on Advanced Applied Informatics (IIAI-AAI). IEEE (2017)
19. Zhou, Y., et al.: Personalized learning full-path recommendation model based on LSTM neural networks. Inf. Sci. 444, 135–152 (2018)
20. Wu, D., Lu, J., Zhang, G.: A fuzzy tree matching-based personalized e-learning recommender system. IEEE Trans. Fuzzy Syst. 23(6), 2412–2426 (2015)
21. Harper, F.M., Konstan, J.A.: The movielens datasets: history and context. ACM Trans. Interact. Intell. Syst. 5(4), 19 (2016)

22. Fenza, G., Orciuoli, F., Sampson, D.G.: Building adaptive tutoring model using artificial neural networks and reinforcement learning. In: 2017 IEEE 17th International Conference on Advanced Learning Technologies (ICALT). IEEE (2017)

23. Al-Hmouz, A., et al.: Modeling and simulation of an adaptive neuro-fuzzy inference system (ANFIS) for mobile learning. IEEE Trans. Learn. Technol. 5(3), 226–237 (2012)

24. Dorça, F.A., et al.: An approach for automatic and dynamic analysis of learning objects repositories through ontologies and data mining techniques for supporting personalized recommendation of content in adaptive and intelligent educational systems. In: 2017 IEEE 17th International Conference on Advanced Learning Technologies (ICALT). IEEE (2017)

25. Yang, T.-Y., et al.: Behavior-based grade prediction for MOOCs via time series neural networks. IEEE J. Sel. Topics Signal Process. 11(5), 716–728 (2017)

26. Brinton, C.G., et al.: Mining MOOC clickstreams: on the relationship between learner behavior and performance. arXiv preprint arXiv:1503.06489 (2015)

27. Brinton, C.G., Chiang, M.: MOOC performance prediction via clickstream data and social learning networks. In: 2015 IEEE Conference on Computer Communications (INFOCOM). IEEE (2015)

28. Chiang, M.: Networks: friends, money, and bytes, Princeton University (2012). https://www.coursera.org/course/friendsmoneybytes

29. Brinton, C., Chiang, M.: Networks illustrated: principles without calculus, Princeton University (2013). https://www.coursera.org/learn/networks-illustrated

30. Kórösi, G., et al.: Clickstream-based outcome prediction in short video MOOCs. In: 2018 International Conference on Computer, Information and Telecommunication Systems (CITS). IEEE (2018)

31. Shridharan, M.: et al.: Predictive learning analytics for video-watching behavior in MOOCs. In: 2018 52nd Annual Conference on Information Sciences and Systems (CISS). IEEE (2018)

32. Sinha, T., et al.: Your click decides your fate: inferring information processing and attrition behavior from MOOC video clickstream interactions. arXiv preprint arXiv:1407.7131 (2014)

33. Odersky, M.: Functional programming principles in scala (2012). https://www.coursera.org/learn/progfun1

34. Lopez, G., et al.: Google BigQuery for education: framework for parsing and analyzing edX MOOC data. In: Proceedings of the Fourth (2017) ACM Conference on Learning@ Scale. ACM (2017)

Personalized Service Recommendation Based on User Dynamic Preferences

Benjamin A. Kwapong$^{(\boxtimes)}$, Richard Anarfi, and Kenneth K. Fletcher [ID]

University of Massachusetts Boston, Boston, MA 02125, USA
{benjamin.kwapong001,richard.anarfi001,kenneth.fletcher}@umb.edu

Abstract. In order to personalize users' recommendations, it is essential to consider their personalized preferences on non-functional attributes during service recommendation. However, to increase recommendation accuracy, it is essential that recommendation systems include users' evolving preferences. It is not sufficient to only consider users' preferences at a point in time. Existing time-based recommendation systems either disregard rich and useful historical user invocation information, or rely on information from similar users, and thus, fail to thoroughly capture users' dynamic preferences for personalized recommendation. This work proposes a method to personalize users' recommendations based on their dynamic preferences on non-functional attributes. First, we compose a user's preference profile as a time series of his/her invocation preference and pre-invocation dependencies (i.e. the different services that were viewed prior to invoking the preferred service). We model a user's invocation preference as a combination of non-functional attribute values observed during service invocation, and topic distribution from WSDL of the invoked service using Hierarchical Dirichlet Process (HDP). Next, we employ long short-term memory recurrent neural networks (LSTM-RNN) to predict the user's future invocation preference. Finally, based on the predicted future invocation preference, we recommend service(s) to that user. To evaluate our proposed method, we perform experiments using real-world service dataset, WS-Dream.

Keywords: Service recommendation · User preference profile ·
LSTM-RNN · User preference evolution · Topic modeling · HDP

1 Introduction

Recommendation systems are attracting much attention because they provide users with prior knowledge of candidate choices to deal with information overload on the Web [1,2]. Most traditional personalized preference-based recommendation systems usually consider user's preferences at a point in time during service recommendation [1–6]. However, it is important to note that, typical user preferences change over time. It is therefore essential to incorporate users' dynamic preferences to provide accurate and timely personalized recommendations [7].

© Springer Nature Switzerland AG 2019
J. E. Ferreira et al. (Eds.): SCC 2019, LNCS 11515, pp. 77–91, 2019.
https://doi.org/10.1007/978-3-030-23554-3_6

For recommendation systems to provide personalized recommendations to users, they must provide a way to: (1) accurately capture and model user dynamic personalized preferences on non-functional attributes, (2) accurately predict user future preferences, and (3) recommend relevant service(s) that satisfies user dynamic preferences. Capturing user dynamic preferences on non-functional attributes is challenging. Some existing works, that have attempted to do so, have utilized either a session-based [8] or a time-series approach [3,7]. In these works, topic modeling such as Latent Dirichlet Allocation (LDA) [9] are used to mine topic distributions from service description documents for a user profile. However, LDA suffers from low efficiency, excessively long training time and low accuracy, especially in applications where the input document is relatively short.

There are some methods that use traditional recurrent neural networks (RNN) to infer user's future preferences for service recommendation [10,11]. These methods, however, suffer from vanishing and exploding gradient issue inherent with RNNs when user historical data in sequence gets larger [12]. Others use various linear predictors based on traditional statistical techniques, such as Autoregressive Moving Average and Autoregressive Integrated Moving Average [13,14], and Gaussian Process [7] algorithms. These time series regression approaches are very sensitive to outliers and depend on an unchanged cause and effect relationships which makes them unsuitable to predict user future dynamic preferences.

To address these limitations and provide accurate personalized recommendations, this work proposes a method that employs Hierarchical Dirichlet Process (HDP) [15,16] and long short-term memory RNN (LSTM-RNN) [12] to capture and predict user preferences for service recommendation. HDP and LSTM-RNN deals with the limitations introduced by LDA and regression methods respectively. The main contributions of this work are summarized as follows:

1. We model a user's invocation preference as a combination of a set of topic distribution, obtained from WSDL and non-functional attribute values, that were observed when that user invoked a service. We employ HDP to extract the topic distribution from the WSDL of the invoked service. In addition, we obtain topic distribution from all WSDL documents from the user's pre-invocation services (i.e. the different service(s) that were viewed prior to invoking the preferred service). This is to establish a relationship between user's intent and invoked service(s). We then aggregate invocation preferences at each timestamp to build a time series of that user's preference profile, which depicts the changes in his/her preferences.

2. Using the user's preference profile, we apply LSTM-RNN to learn and predict his/her future invocation preference, i.e. the topic distribution and non-functional attribute values of a prospective service. To recommend top-K services, we compute the similarity between the user's future non-functional attribute and candidate services. This similarity value is then used as weights in the weighted Jensen-Shannon Divergence [17] to compute the similarity

between user's future invocation preference and topic distribution of candidate services. Top-ranked services are then recommended to the user.
3. We perform a series of experiments using real-world services, WS-Dream [18], to evaluate and validate our proposed method.

The rest of the paper is outlined as follows. In Sect. 2 we discuss some of the notable and significant service recommendation works based on user dynamic preference. We present our proposed LSTM-RNN method in detail in Sect. 3 followed by our experiments, evaluations and analysis in Sect. 4. Finally, we conclude our paper and discuss some of the open ended challenges as a part of our future work in Sect. 5.

2   Related Work

To the best of our knowledge, this is the first recommendation technique that models user invocation preference to include non-functional attributes and topic distribution from WSDL documents extracted from user invocation and pre-invocation services history. However, the idea of personalized service recommendation and the importance of user intent has been exploited in some research areas. Wu et al. [19] employs a deep recurrent neural network approach to exploit current viewing history of the user to improve recommendation accuracy. The main difference between their work and our proposed method is that they failed to consider a user's pre-invocation services history during service recommendation. In addition, their method employed collaborative filtering approach, which primarily rely on information from similar users/items, thus failing to build personalized models for individual users with rich past information [7]. Other related personalized recommendation models [20,21] also employ collaborative filtering to make their recommendations.

Our use of topic modeling from user service invocations and pre-invocation services is similar to the work of Liu [7] and Uetsuji et al. [22]. In her work, Liu [7] proposed a method that uses LDA to model user's preferences and then applied the Gaussian Process to predict user's future preference. Uetsuji et al. [22] considered capturing user's intent in effecting service recommendation by using a topic tracking model. A customer's behavior was generated in a two-step probabilistic process; in the first step a topic was selected according to a topic probability distribution representing topic selection tendency. Then, in the next step the user's activity is determined according to activity probability distribution linked to the selected topic in the first step. They however trained their model using a probabilistic expectation maximization algorithm, which estimates parameters in statistical models. The importance of user intent in recommendation systems was further highlighted by Bhattacharya et al. [4]. They use tensor factorization techniques to encode user activity and then create an intent score. A combination of the intent score and contextual information produces recommendation scores. These recommendation scores are ranked through filtering and collaborative recommendation techniques. The methods in this work largely focus on probabilistic statistical models and therefore also have limitations of statistical regression mentioned in Sect. 1.

Another key consideration for service recommender systems is the concept of user preference evolution in user preference modeling. This essential because user preferences over time are rather dynamic than static. This renders traditional recommender systems, which considers user preferences at a point in time, less accurate as time unfolds and user preferences evolve. Zhou et al. [17], in their work, highlighted on the lack of automatic adaptiveness of the traditional user modeling systems to the dynamic nature of user preferences. They approached this problem by analyzing the characteristics of memory through ZGrapher. They then employed a Forgetting and Re-energizing User Preference (FRUP) algorithm to trace the user preferences. These preferences are divided into long-term, medium-term and short-term for the accurate description of memory patterns in different scenarios. In our work, however, we do not categorize the preferences into short or long term based on the premise that user preferences are dynamic. A short term preference could easily become a long term one and vice versa based on user preference evolution. Our model automatically captures these user dynamics by learning from the user's past invocations and pre-invocation dependencies.

Aside our difference in approach, the use of RNN has been exploited in other related service recommendation works [10, 11, 23]. These researchers, have leveraged the strength of RNN in handling a sequence of input data to fully capture user intent, patterns and behavior to accurately model the user profiles. Xia et al. [10] explores the provision of an explainable recommendation based on the sequential check-in data of the user. In their work, they make use of sequential check-in data to capture users' life pattern and intent, to describe the user's personal preference. They then employ a RNN, which they qualify as attention-based, to make a series of recommendations instead of simply showing top-N recommendations. RNNs have been applied to recommendation systems in the movie industry Chu et al. [11]. Here, they highlight the inability for collaborative filtering techniques to handle user changing habits. They subsequently built a prediction model based on RNN to handle the temporal factor of user interests. Their model treats a user's recent ratings or behavior as a sequence with each hidden layer modeling a user's rating or behavior in order. Li et al. [23] proposed a method for automatic Hashtag recommendation of new tweets. They used a skip-gram model to generate distributed word representations and then initially applied a convolutional neural network to learn semantic sentence vectors. After this, they made use of the sentence vectors to train a long short-term memory recurrent neural network (LSTM-RNN) and used the produced tweet vectors as features to classify hashtags.

3   Proposed Personalized Service Recommendation Based on User Dynamic Preferences

This section first discusses an overview of our proposed method and subsequently describes the main modules (engines) that drives our method. Figure 1 shows an overview of our proposed method. The three main engines are:

1. User preference profile engine: Based on the Hierarchical Dirichlet Process (HDP) [15], this engine is responsible for creating user preference profile, which is a time series of the user's invocation;
2. LSTM-RNN prediction engine: Takes user preference profile as an input and based on a transformation function, predicts its future invocation preference; and
3. Service ranking engine: Ranks services by computing similarity between future invocation preference and candidate services. The similarity function is based on weighted Jensen-Shannon Divergence [17]. Top-ranked services are then recommended to the user.

Details of each of these engines are described in the sections that follow.

3.1   Problem Definition

Let $U = \{u_1, u_2, ..., u_e\}$ be a set of users and $S = \{s_1, s_2, ..., s_f\}$ be a set of services. For each $s \in S$, there is a set of non-functional attributes, Q, that describe the service s. When a user $u \in U$ invokes a service $s \in S$, we record the user's invocation preference as a tuple:

$$I_s^u = < \Lambda, \breve{Q}, \Omega > \tag{1}$$

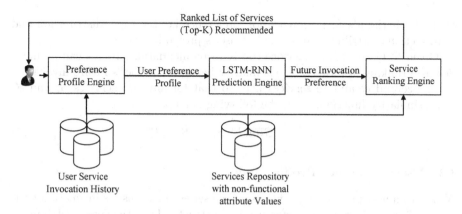

Fig. 1. Overview of the proposed LSTM-RNN method for personalized service recommendation based on user dynamic preferences

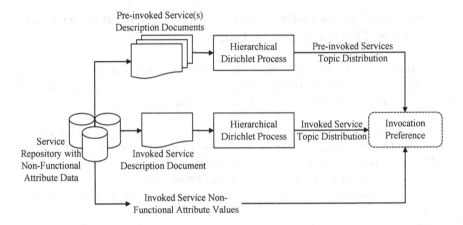

Fig. 2. User invocation preference process

where $\varLambda = \{\lambda_1, \lambda_2, ..., \lambda_n\}$ is the topic distribution extracted from the WSDL document of s, $\check{Q} = \{\check{q}_1, \check{q}_2, ..., \check{q}_m\}$ is the set of non-functional attribute values observed when s was invoked, and $\varOmega = \{\omega_1, \omega_2, ..., \omega_k\}$ is the set of topic distribution recognized from $u's$ activities prior to invoking s. We model a user $u's$ preference profile P_u as a time series of his/her invocation preferences as:

$$P_u = \{I^u_{\bar{S}}(t), t = 0, 1, 2, ...\} \tag{2}$$

where $\bar{S} \subset S$.

Given a user $u's$ preference profile, P_u, we predict the user's future invocation preference on a probable service $\tilde{s} \in S$, using LSTM-RNN as:

$$f(P_u) :\longrightarrow \hat{I}^u_{\tilde{s}} \tag{3}$$

where $\hat{I}^u_{\tilde{s}}$, is the $u's$ future invocation preference i.e. the topic distribution and non-functional attribute values of that user's probable service.

Given S, Q and $\hat{I}^u_{\tilde{s}}$, the service top-K recommendation process can be modeled as a ranking in terms of the similarity between the user's future invocation preference and candidate services [24], so that for any two services S_i and S_j and a similarity function, Sim, the following is true.

$$S_i \succ S_j \Longleftrightarrow Sim(\hat{I}^u_{\tilde{s}}, S_i) \leq Sim(\hat{I}^u_{\tilde{s}}, S_j) \tag{4}$$

3.2   User Preference Profile Model

We model a user preference profile as a time series of that user's invocation preference. A user's invocation preference is constructed from the topic distribution obtained from the WSDL document together with the non-functional attribute values of the invoked service. We also include the topic distribution of all services a user visits prior to invoking the preferred service. Figure 2 describes the user invocation preference process. When a user u invokes a service s, we associate the service invocation WSDL document, W_s and non-functional attribute, $\check{Q}$. Using this document as a corpus, we employ HDP to extract topics such that each word in the document has the probability of being assigned to a topic and each W_s is associated to a topic distribution Λ. We then append $\check{Q}$ to Λ_s. We complete $u's$ invocation preference I by also adding the topic distribution of all $u's$ service interactions, Ω. To build $u's$ preference profile, we sort all invocation preferences by timestamp, in a chronological order and model each invocation preference with time as a time series (see Fig. 3).

User preference profile involves topic distribution modeling. Lately, probabilistic topic models such as Latent Dirichlet Allocation (LDA) [9], have been applied to extract and represent users' preference in different application scenarios [7]. LDA has been applied successfully to identify topics in documents and discover implicit semantic correlation among those documents. However, it suffers from low efficiency, excessively long training time and low accuracy, especially in applications where the input document is relatively short (e.g. WSDL document). Due to these limitations, we employ HDP for our topic modeling.

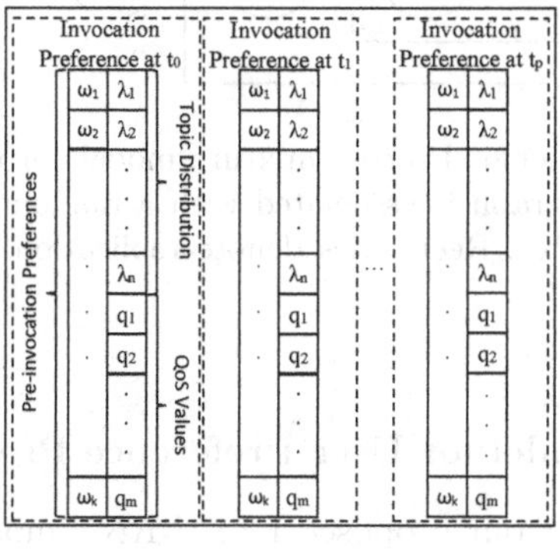

Fig. 3. User preference profile

HDP, an extension of LDA, is a multi-layer form of the Dirichlet Process (DP), designed to address cases in topic document modeling where the number of topic terms is not known in advance. For each document, a mixture of topics are drawn from a Dirichlet distribution, and then each word in the document is treated as an independent draw from that mixture [15]. Figure 4 shows a graphical model formalism of HDP. The global measure, G_0 is distributed as a Dirichlet Process (DP) with concentration parameter γ and base probability measure H:

$$G_0 \mid \gamma, H \sim DP(\gamma, H) \tag{5}$$

and the random measures G_j are conditionally independent given G_0, with distributions given by a Dirichlet Process with base probability measure G_0:

$$G_j \mid \alpha_0, G_0 \sim DP(\alpha_0, G_0) \tag{6}$$

The hyperparameters of the Hierarchical Dirichlet Process consist of the baseline probability measure H, and the concentration parameters γ and α_0. The baseline H provides the prior distribution for the topic of the ith word in the jth WSDL document, θ_{ji}. For each j let $\theta_{j1}, \theta_{j2}, ...$ be independent and identically distributed random topics distributed as G_j. Each θ_{ji} is a topic corresponding to a single observation x_{ji}. The likelihood is given by:

$$\theta_{ji} \mid G_j \sim G_j$$

$$x_{ji} \mid \theta_{ji} \sim F(\theta_{ji}) \tag{7}$$

which is the Hierarchical Dirichlet Process mixture model [15].

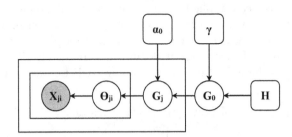

Fig. 4. A Hierarchical Dirichlet Process mixture model. In the graphical model formalism, each node in the graph is associated with a random variable, where shading denotes an observed variable. Rectangles denote replication of the model within the rectangle [15].

3.3   LSTM-RNN Model for User Preference Prediction

In this section, we discuss our proposed LSTM-RNN model. A recurrent neural network (RNN) is a type of artificial neural network (ANN) designed to recognize patterns in sequences of data [11]. Unlike traditional Neural Networks, which assume that all inputs and outputs are independent of each other, RNNs make use of sequential information. RNNs use their internal state to capture information that has been previously calculated, based on which the next item in the sequence is predicted. RNNs use back propagation algorithm [11], applied for every time stamp and this is commonly known as back propagation through time (BPTT). BPTT, however, introduces vanishing gradient and exploding gradient issues in RNN, when the number of items in the sequence gets large (long term dependencies) [12]. These limitations can be resolved by Long Short-Term Memory networks (LSTM), which we will employ in this work. LSTM are a special kind of RNN, capable of learning long-term dependencies. They were introduced by Hochreiter and Schmidhuber [12] and were refined and popularized by many people in following work [25–28]. An LSTM is composed of a cell, an input gate, an output gate and a forget gate. The major component is the cell state ("memory") which runs through the entire chain with occasional information updates from the input(add) and forget(remove) gates. An LSTM network computes a mapping from an input sequence $x = (x_1, ..., x_T)$ to an output sequence $y = (y_1, ..., y_T)$ by calculating the network unit activations using the following equations iteratively from $t = 1$ to T [29]:

$$i_t = \sigma(W_{ix}x_t + W_{im}m_{t-1} + W_{ic}c_t + b_i) \tag{8}$$

$$f_t = \sigma(W_{fx}x_t + W_{fm}m_{t-1} + W_{fc}c_{t-1} + b_f) \tag{9}$$

$$c_t = f_t \odot c_{t-1} + i_t \odot g(W_{cx}x_t + W_{cm}m_{t-1} + b_c) \tag{10}$$

$$o_t = \sigma(w_{ox}x_t + W_{om}m_{t-1} + W_{oc}c_t + b_o) \tag{11}$$

$$m_t = o_t \odot h(c_t) \tag{12}$$

$$y_t = \phi(W_{ym}m_t + b_y) \tag{13}$$

Fig. 5. Encoder-decoder LSTM architecture

- f: forget gate's activation vector
- i: input gate's activation vector
- o: output gate's activation vector
- h: output vector of the LSTM unit
- g: cell input activation function, generally tanh
- h: cell output activation functions, generally tanh
- c: cell activation vector
- W: weight matrices parameters
- b: bias vector parameters
- $\odot$: element-wise product of the vectors
- σ: the logistic sigmoid function
- ϕ: the network output activation function

We model our predicting function by using the encoder-decoder LSTM architecture [23], which is comprised of two models: the first is to read the input sequence and encode it into a fixed-length vector, and the second for decoding the fixed-length vector and outputting the predicted sequence. Figure 5 shows a simplified diagram of an encoder-decoder LSTM. Our prediction model takes as input, the invocation preference at the various timestamps $(t_0, t_1, t_2, ..., t_n)$ and predicts as output, the future user invocation preference at time t_{n+1}.

In this work, we use one LSTM to implement the encoder model and another LSTM for the decoder model. The encoder learns the relationship between the steps in the input sequence and develop an internal representation of those relationships. The decoder then transforms the learned internal representation of the input sequence into the correct output sequence. Figure 6 shows a basic representation of our sequence to sequence model with encoder-decoder LSTM.

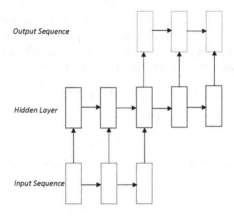

Output Sequence

Hidden Layer

Input Sequence

Fig. 6. Many-to-many RNN

3.4 Service Recommendation

To recommend a service to a user u, we calculate the weighed Jensen-Shannon divergence [30] between u's future invocation preference and the topic distribution of each candidate service using non-functional attribute values as weights. Given two normalized distributions $t_j = \{t_j^1, t_j^2, .., t_j^K\}$ and $r_j = \{r_j^1, r_j^2, .., r_j^K\}$, where K is the number of the bins in each histogram. Then the Jensen-Shannon Divergence (JSD) between t_j and r_j can be defined as:

$$JSD(r_j\|t_j) = \frac{1}{2}KLD(r_j\|m_j) + \frac{1}{2}KLD(t_j\|m_j) \tag{14}$$

$$KLD(r_j\|m_j) = \sum_{k=1}^{K} r_j^k log \frac{r_j^k}{m_j^k} \tag{15}$$

where $m_j = \frac{1}{2}(r_j + t_j)$.

For a JSD, it is alway necessary to select the hypothesis that produces smaller differences between the ideal and predicted distributions. Hence, the residual distribution is weighed using non-functional attribute values generated in a standard Gaussian function $g = \{g^1, g^2, ..., g^K\}$ ($\mu = 0, \sigma2 = 1$) to generate the Gaussian-weighted JSD (GJSD) [30]. The Gaussian weight function reinforces the influence of JSD for data points. GJSD is formulated as:

$$GJSD(r_j\|t_j) = \frac{1}{2}GKLD(r_j\|m_j) + \frac{1}{2}GKLD(t_j\|m_j) \tag{16}$$

$$GKLD(r_j\|m_j) = \sum_{k=1}^{K} g^k r_j^k log \frac{r_j^k}{m_j^k} \tag{17}$$

4   Experiments and Results

This section describes the experiments we conducted we conducted to evaluate
and validate our proposed LSTM-RNN method for personalized service recommendation based on user dynamic preference. We also discuss our results.

4.1   Experimental Setup and Dataset Description

Our experiments were performed on WS-Dream dataset [18], a real-world web
service quality of service performance dataset. The data set contains about 2
million web service invocation records of 5,825 web services with about 339 users.
It contains the response time and throughput values for all invoked services. We
visited all the WSDL addresses in the dataset and out of the 5,825 web services,
3,544 were found to be valid. Therefore, we conducted our experiments with
these valid services.

From the 3,544 valid services, we identified 294 different groups of services
based on their similar WSDL addresses. For each group of n valid services, we
chose the first $1..n-1$ and designated those as pre-invocation dependencies while
the nth service was designated as the invoked service. Based on this, we used
HDP to generate topic distributions and user profiles (timestamps of invocation preferences). We subsequently split the 294 different groups of services into
training, testing and validating sets for experiments.

4.2   Performance Metric

To quantitatively assess the overall performance of our LSTM-RNN model, Mean
Square Error (MSE) was used to estimate the prediction accuracy. MSE is a scale
dependent metric which quantifies the difference between the predicted values
and the actual values of the quantity being predicted by computing the average
sum of squared errors:

$$MSE = \frac{1}{N} \sum_{N=1}^{N} (y_i - \hat{y}_i)^2 \tag{18}$$

where y_i is the observed value, $\hat{y}_i$ is the predicted value and N represents the
total number of predictions.

4.3   Results

We conducted our experiment with two RNN based encoder-decoder models of
LSTM and Gated Recurrent Unit (GRU). The experiments were ran over 25
epochs for both models with 256 memory cells each for encoder and decoder
models. We employed *rmsprop* as optimizer and used *categorical crossentropy*
as the loss function for our LSTM and GRU models. Figures 7a and b show an
overlay distribution and a cumulative ogive of predicted and expected respectively. From these two figures, we observe that our trained model is sensitive to

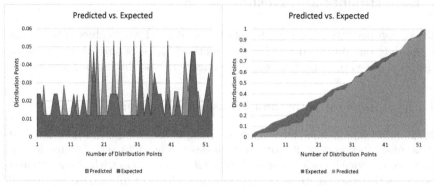

(a) Distribution overlay   (b) Cumulative distribution ogive

Fig. 7. Comparison between predicted and expected distributions

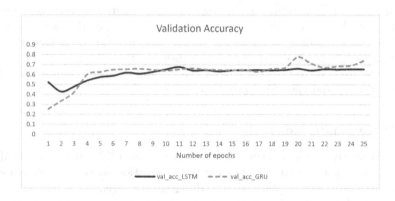

Fig. 8. Validation accuracy over 25 epochs for LSTM and GRU

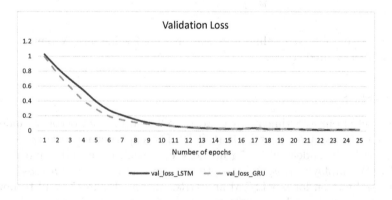

Fig. 9. Validation loss over 25 epochs for LSTM and GRU

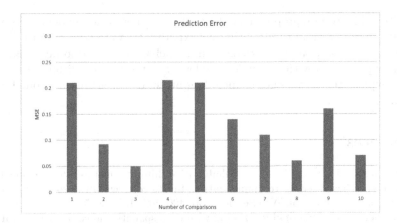

Fig. 10. MSE of predicted and expected distributions

some distribution data points in our test set. This, we attribute to the dataset on which we trained our model with. The graphs of validation accuracy and validation loss of the LSTM and GRU are shown in Figs. 8 and 9 respectively. It is evident from Fig. 8 that the performances of LSTMs and GRUs for our experiment were comparable. This comes as no surprise as both LSTMs and GRUs use memory to ensure that the gradient can pass across many time steps without vanishing or exploding. We also checked the accuracy of our prediction. For this experiment, the predicted distribution from our model is compared to the expected distribution and the MSE recorded. Figure 10 shows different error rates that we obtained for the 10 predictions we validated.

5 Conclusion and Future Work

Giving personalized recommendations is a very essential task for business and individuals alike. However, to increase recommendation accuracy, it is essential that recommendation systems include users' evolving preferences. It is not sufficient to only consider users' preferences at a point in time because user preferences change with time. In addition, users leave behind rich and useful historical invocation information, that could be employed to improve recommendation accuracy. In this work, we have proposed a method to personalize users' recommendations based on their dynamic preferences on non-functional attributes. Our proposed model creates a user preference profile as a time series of his/her invocation preference and pre-invocation dependencies (i.e. the different services that were viewed prior to invoking the preferred service). In our work, we also modeled a user's invocation preference as a combination of non-functional attribute values observed during service invocation, and topic distribution from WSDL of the invoked service using Hierarchical Dirichlet Process (HDP). We employed long short-term memory recurrent neural networks (LSTM-RNN) to predict the user's future invocation preference to recommend service(s) to that user. To evaluate our proposed method, we have performed experiments with WS-Dream dataset and results from our experiments were very promising.

As future work, we will expand our model in a new hypothesis and run several experiments with a couple of relevant datasets. Specifically, we would like to explore the advantages of including attention mechanisms in our LSTM model.

References

1. Fletcher, K.K., Liu, X.F.: A collaborative filtering method for personalized preference-based service recommendation. In: Proceedings of the 2015 IEEE International Conference on Web Services, pp. 400–407, June 2015
2. Fletcher, K.K.: A method for dealing with data sparsity and cold-start limitations in service recommendation using personalized preferences. In: 2017 IEEE International Conference on Cognitive Computing (ICCC), pp. 72–79, June 2017
3. Cao, B., Liu, X., Rahman, M.M., Li, B., Liu, J., Tang, M.: Integrated content and network-based service clustering and web APIs recommendation for mashup development. IEEE Trans. Serv. Comput. **PP**(99), 1 (2017)
4. Bhattacharya, B., Burhanuddin, I., Sancheti, A., Satya, K.: Intent-aware contextual recommendation system. In: 2017 IEEE International Conference on Data Mining Workshops (ICDMW), pp. 1–8, November 2017
5. Zheng, Z., Ma, H., Lyu, M.R., King, I.: Qos-aware web service recommendation by collaborative filtering. IEEE Trans. Serv. Comput. **4**(2), 140–152 (2011)
6. Chen, X., Zheng, Z., Liu, X., Huang, Z., Sun, H.: Personalized QoS-aware web service recommendation and visualization. IEEE Trans. Serv. Comput. **6**(1), 35–47 (2013)
7. Liu, X.: Modeling users' dynamic preference for personalized recommendation. In: Proceedings of the 24th International Conference on Artificial Intelligence. IJCAI 2015, pp. 1785–1791. AAAI Press (2015)
8. Quadrana, M., Karatzoglou, A., Hidasi, B., Cremonesi, P.: Personalizing session-based recommendations with hierarchical recurrent neural networks. In: Proceedings of the Eleventh ACM Conference on Recommender Systems, RecSys 2017, pp. 130–137. ACM, New York (2017)
9. Blei, D.M., Ng, A.Y., Jordan, M.I.: Latent dirichlet allocation. J. Mach. Learn. Res. **3**, 993–1022 (2003)
10. Xia, B., Li, Y., Li, Q., Li, T.: Attention-based recurrent neural network for location recommendation. In: 2017 12th International Conference on Intelligent Systems and Knowledge Engineering (ISKE), pp. 1–6, November 2017
11. Chu, Y., Huang, F., Wang, H., Li, G., Song, X.: Short-term recommendation with recurrent neural networks. In: 2017 IEEE International Conference on Mechatronics and Automation (ICMA), pp. 927–932, August 2017
12. Hochreiter, S., Schmidhuber, J.: Long short-term memory. Neural Comput. **9**(8), 1735–1780 (1997)
13. Azzouni, A., Pujolle, G.: A long short-term memory recurrent neural network framework for network traffic matrix prediction. CoRR abs/1705.05690 (2017)
14. Dai, J., Li, J.: VBR MPEG video traffic dynamic prediction based on the modeling and forecast of time series. In: 2009 Fifth International Joint Conference on INC, IMS and IDC, pp. 1752–1757, August 2009

15. Teh, Y.W., Jordan, M.I., Beal, M.J., Blei, D.M.: Hierarchical Dirichlet processes. J. Am. Stat. Assoc. **101**, 1566–1581 (2004)
16. Fletcher, K.K.: A quality-based web API selection for mashup development using affinity propagation. In: Ferreira, J.E., Spanoudakis, G., Ma, Y., Zhang, L.-J. (eds.) SCC 2018. LNCS, vol. 10969, pp. 153–165. Springer, Cham (2018). https://doi.org/10.1007/978-3-319-94376-3_10
17. Zhou, B., Zhang, B., Liu, Y., Xing, K.: User model evolution algorithm: Forgetting and reenergizing user preference. In: 2011 International Conference on Internet of Things and 4th International Conference on Cyber, Physical and Social Computing, pp. 444–447, October 2011
18. Zheng, Z., Ma, H., Lyu, M.R., King, I.: WSRec: a collaborative filtering based web service recommender system. In: 2009 IEEE International Conference on Web Services, pp. 437–444, July 2009
19. Wu, S., Ren, W., Yu, C., Chen, G., Zhang, D., Zhu, J.: Personal recommendation using deep recurrent neural networks in NetEase. In: 2016 IEEE 32nd International Conference on Data Engineering (ICDE), pp. 1218–1229, May 2016
20. Qing-ji, T., Hao, W., Cong, W., Qi, G.: A personalized hybrid recommendation strategy based on user behaviors and its application. In: 2017 International Conference on Security, Pattern Analysis, and Cybernetics (SPAC), pp. 181–186, December 2017
21. Xing, L., Ma, Q., Chen, S.: A novel personalized recommendation model based on location computing. In: 2017 Chinese Automation Congress (CAC), pp. 3355–3359, October 2017
22. Uetsuji, K., Yanagimoto, H., Yoshioka, M.: User intent estimation from access logs with topic model. In: 19th International Conference on Knowledge Based and Intelligent Information and Engineering Systems, pp. 141–149 (2015)
23. Li, J., Xu, H., He, X., Deng, J., Sun, X.: Tweet modeling with LSTM recurrent neural networks for hashtag recommendation. In: 2016 International Joint Conference on Neural Networks (IJCNN), pp. 1570–1577, July 2016
24. Fletcher, K.: A method for aggregating ranked services for personal preference based selection. Int. J. Web Serv. Res. (IJWSR) **16**(2), 1–23 (2019)
25. Gers, F.A., Schmidhuber, J., Cummins, F.: Learning to forget: continual prediction with LSTM. In: 1999 Ninth International Conference on Artificial Neural Networks ICANN 1999 (Conf. Publ. No. 470), vol. 2, pp. 850–855 (1999)
26. Graves, A., Schmidhuber, J.: Framewise phoneme classification with bidirectional LSTM networks. In: Proceedings. 2005 IEEE International Joint Conference on Neural Networks, vol. 4, pp. 2047–2052, July 2005
27. Wollmer, M., Eyben, F., Keshet, J., Graves, A., Schuller, B., Rigoll, G.: Robust discriminative keyword spotting for emotionally colored spontaneous speech using bidirectional LSTM networks. In: 2009 IEEE International Conference on Acoustics, Speech and Signal Processing, pp. 3949–3952, April 2009
28. Graves, A., Jaitly, N., Mohamed, A.R.: Hybrid speech recognition with deep bidirectional LSTM. In: 2013 IEEE Workshop on Automatic Speech Recognition and Understanding, pp. 273–278, December 2013
29. Sak, H., Senior, A., Beaufays, F.: Long short-term memory recurrent neural network architectures for large scale acoustic modeling. In: INTERSPEECH 2014, 15th Annual Conference of the International Speech Communication Association, Singapore, 14–18 September 2014, pp. 338–342, September 2014
30. Zhou, K., Varadarajan, K.M., Zillich, M., Vincze, M.: Gaussian-weighted Jensen-Shannon divergence as a robust fitness function for multi-model fitting. Mach. Vis. Appl. **24**(6), 1107–1119 (2013)

Toward Better Service Performance Management via Workload Prediction

Hachem Moussa[1]($\boxtimes$) ⬚, I-Ling Yen[1], Farokh Bastani[1], Yulin Dong[2], and Wei He[2]

[1] University of Texas at Dallas, Dallas, TX 75080, USA
hxm036000@utdallas.edu
[2] Shandong University, Shandong, China

Abstract. In this paper, we consider managing service performance starting from the composition time, aiming to reduce the risk of execution failures during service composition. We use ARIMA to predict workloads of the services at the time when they are likely to be invoked and subsequently predict the response time and chances that the requests for accessing the services may be declined due to admission control. The in-depth analysis can help avoid timing failures during service execution. However, these analyses may incur overhead and we introduce a two-phase composition algorithm to reduce the potential overhead. Our system also considers continuous monitoring and service recomposition to greatly increase the probability of completing the service execution within the deadline. Experimental results show that our service management approach can greatly improve the success rate for meeting the deadline.

Keywords: Service performance · Performance management ·
Service composition · Service execution · Workload prediction

1 Introduction

The first step toward managing the performance of a composite service execution is to perform careful timing analysis during service composition. Service composition for satisfying timing requirements have been explored extensively. Earlier works assume that each web service has a constant response time [1], which is unrealistic since the workloads of service host can significantly impact the service response time. Frequently, even assuming such a constant response time as the worst case scenario will not help because if the service host does not control the service request arrival rate, the arrival can saturate the service and result in unbounded service time. This scenario brings up the need for admission control. However, admission control itself presents a severe issue in QoS-aware service composition. Consider a composite workflow that is composed without considering potential admission control. When a request to an atomic concrete service in the composite workflow is declined by the selected service provider due to the admission control of the provider, the composite service composed originally will fail. Thus, besides considering the workload, considering the admission control policies of the service providers are also very critical.

© Springer Nature Switzerland AG 2019
J. E. Ferreira et al. (Eds.): SCC 2019, LNCS 11515, pp. 92–106, 2019.
https://doi.org/10.1007/978-3-030-23554-3_7

In the attempt to solve the issues of meeting the timing requirements for service requests, there have been works on adjusting the resource allocation for each service in an attempt to maintain a level of QoS of the service [5–7]. However, these approaches cannot guarantee bounded service time either, unless the arrival rate of the service requests is bounded. This goes back to the admission control issue. Therefore, even though dynamic resource management methods are very important in providing assured service response time, they still have problems and limitations.

When considering service performance management, it is essential to consider continuous monitoring and dynamic service recomposition [2, 3] to cope with the problem of service execution time failures. However, upon the detection of failures, the reactive time may not be sufficient to allow the successful completion of the composite workflow. For example, if a service does not finish within the expected service time due to the over-time execution, then it may be necessary to re-select concrete services to ground the remaining abstract services. If the admission for a concrete service that can offer very good service time guarantee is declined, then the recomposition may fail because the opportunity of selecting different concrete services with lower response time may exist in the earlier services that have already been executed. Moreover, service composition and recomposition do take time. Thus, though it is always necessary to offer continuous monitoring and dynamic recomposition, it is also desirable to have a better composition to start with.

Summarizing the discussion above, the first step toward good service performance management for service-based systems is to consider more comprehensive timing analysis during service composition. Existing works in QoS-aware service composition do not comprehensively address the impact of workload and admission control of concrete services. In this paper, we focus on improving timing analysis at the composition time to achieve a better composition that, during execution, has a higher probability to satisfy the given timing constraints. We will simply use the solutions given in the literature for continuous monitoring, management, and dynamic recomposition to further avoid the violation of timing requirements in composite service execution.

To achieve the goal, we consider (a) derive more accurate timing properties for the candidate concrete services in the workflow by estimating the workloads of the providers, and (b) consider admission control at composition time to ensure that the composite service will not fail during execution because the concrete service cannot admit it. Since performing more accurate timing analysis may increase the overhead of the composition process, we also consider (c) a two-phase algorithm to reduce the overhead.

Note that when performing workload prediction for (a), we should not consider predicting the current workload, but should predict the workload at the time the service is to be invoked. Consider a service chain (one path) in a workflow, $s_1, \ldots, s_{i-1}, s_i, \ldots$, where will be executed after s_i to s_{i-1} have finished execution. At that time, s_i's workload may have changed significantly. If s_i to s_{i-1} have relatively long execution time, the problem will become more severe.

For (a), we predict the workloads of the services right at the time they are invoked. Take the earlier example of a service chain, $s_1, s_2, s_3, \ldots$ Evaluating s_3's workload at its invocation time requires the knowledge of the completion time of s_2, which subsequently requires the knowledge of the response time of s_1. We sequentially predict the workloads of the services in the workflow to properly derive their response times and subsequently derive the end-to-end response time of the entire workflow.

Once we predict the workload of a concrete service and if we know the admission control policy of the service provider, we can estimate the risk that the candidate concrete service may decline the service request at the time it is invoked. Based on the estimation, we can greatly reduce the risk of timing failures for service execution.

The fine-grained timing analysis can help better analyze the timing behavior of the candidate compositions, but it also incurs heavy overhead. For (c), We use a two-phase solution to avert the problem. In the first phase, we use conventional QoS-aware service composition algorithm based on genetic algorithm to select K most prominent candidate concrete compositions for an abstract workflow. In the second phase, we use ARIMA (autoregressive integrated moving average) to predict the workload of composite services for each composition candidate in the top K candidate list. The composite services workload prediction is done to accurately derive their response time at their invocation times. Then, end-to-end response time can be derived for the composition candidate. Finally, the candidate composition with the best QoS is selected for grounding. We also use the predicted workload for the composite services to predict whether the service request may be declined due to admission control. Since the fine-grained analysis is only performed on much fewer candidates, the analysis overhead can be justified. To prepare for the potential of analysis errors, the second phase also returns a few alternative candidate compositions with shorter execution times and potentially worse quality in other QoS attributes together with the grounded composition.

We conducted experiments to evaluate our in-depth timing analysis approach for service composition and compare it with conventional solutions in terms of the rate of timing violations. The experimental results show that our scheme can reduce the timing violations without suffering from composition time overhead by selecting a service composition that has a lower chance to fail. Our two-phase approach can greatly improve the composition and achieve a higher success rate of service execution. At the same time, the composition time is also reduced since the lowered failure rate results in reduced chance of recomposition and, therefore, reduced overall composition time.

The rest of the paper is organized as follows. Section 2 discusses the related work. Section 3 introduces the system architecture. Section 4 provides an overview of the ARIMA model and how it is used for workload prediction in our two-phase protocol. Section 5 discusses the two-phase service composition algorithm and how to consider admission control at composition time. The experimental study is presented in Sect. 6 and the results are presented in Sect. 7. Section 8 concludes the paper.

2 Related Work

Some research works consider dynamic composition and re-composition of services to satisfy real time requirements. In [2] a self-healing approach for web service composition is proposed, which selects backup compositions and uses them upon execution time failures. The paper assumes that the web service response time is constant and focuses on the data transmission delays. Dynamic re-composition or dynamically adjusting the parameters of reconfiguration services are essential in real-time SOA, and can be used in conjunction with improved service composition algorithms to achieve higher assurance for real time service execution. In [4], reconfigurable web services are considered in QoS-aware service composition. Each service can be configured on the fly to achieve different execution time by trading off other quality attributes.

There are also research works that consider dynamically adjusting resource allocations for services to satisfy the timing requirements. In [5], multi-tier services are considered and a hybrid queueing model is used to determine the number of virtual machines to be allocated to each service at each tier so that the desired response time can be maintained. [6] allocates resources in cloud environment based on predicted service load. The major focus of the paper is on the framework design for adaptively adjusting the resource provisions for services in the cloud. Similarly, [7] uses a queuing model to determine the optimal resource allocation for services. It also proposes a priority-based scheduling to assure that higher priority tasks can satisfy their real time requirements.

Dynamically adjusting resource allocations to services can help assure the satisfaction of the timing requirement of the composite services. However, guaranteeing response time always requires the request arrival rate to be bounded. Thus, some research works consider admission control to assure bounded request arrival rate [8]. But admission control introduces new issues in service composition because a service request may be declined at execution time, causing a timing failure. None of the existing QoS-aware service composition works consider the potential impact of admission control during service composition and it is specifically considered in this paper.

Various methods have been considered for predicting the execution time of a composite service based on different data sources. [9] uses a model-driven approach and layered queuing network (LQN) to predict the performance of composite web services. [10] also uses LQN to model the layered middleware to predict the overall system performance. In [11], a Hidden Markov Model (HMM) is used to predict whether a composition of cloud service components can satisfy the QoS requirements. [12] proposes to use the time series similarity measure between the predicted QoS values and user requirements to estimate the long-term QoS of a service composition. In [17], we have proposed to use a queuing model for timing analysis of composite services. All these methods are useful in our performance management framework for composite service time prediction, and we choose ARIMA for the purpose.

3   System Architecture

We consider a system where there are decentralized service brokers managing the workflow composition and execution for the clients. The architecture for a service broker B_K is shown in Fig. 1.

A client may submit a composition request $R = \langle awf, QR, st \rangle$ to a service broker B_K through its Request Interface, where awf is the abstract workflow, QR is the QoS requirements for the workflow, and st is the desired starting time for the workflow.

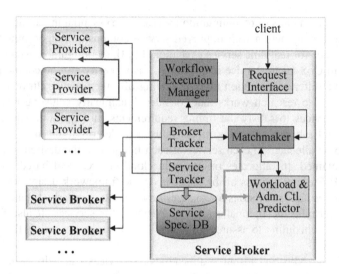

Fig. 1. Service broker architecture for service management

The abstract workflow *awf* includes a set of n abstract services $\{as_1, as_2, \ldots, as_n\}$. $QR = \langle TR, qr_1, \ldots, qr_q \rangle$ is the QoS requirement for *awf*, where TR is the time constraint for *awf* and $qr_i, 1 \leq i \leq q$, are the constraints on other QoS attributes which can be taken care of by many general QoS-aware service composition algorithms. Let *wf* denote the concrete workflow *awf* is grounded to. TR is the maximal expected response time allowed for *wf*, i.e., every path in *wf* should be executed within time TR. To simplify the discussion without loss of generality, we only consider the timing for one path in *awf*. The overall execution time will simply be the maximal execution time among all the paths of *awf*.

B_K has a Service Tracker which keeps track of a set of service providers, obtains the specifications and QoS properties of their concrete services and maintains them in its Service Specification DB. B_K may crawl the web to find new concrete services and add them to the DB. Since it is not possible for each service broker to keep track of all available services, we assume that each broker has some expertise areas and they know almost all the alternative services of the same functionality. The Service Provider, once gets subscribed by a broker, will periodically push the updated service information to the broker, including the current and historical workload (service request arrival rate) of each service it hosts. B_K maintains the current and historical workloads it receives for relevant services and uses the data for workload prediction.

B_K also keeps track of other service brokers and their expertise areas via its Broker Tracker. During service composition for a client request R, if B_K does not host the information for grounding some abstract services of R, say as_i, its Broker Tracker identifies another broker $B_{K'}$, which hosts the concrete services information for as_i, and contacts $B_{K'}$ to obtain the information of the candidate concrete services. It may also request $B_{K'}$ to predict the workload when the data is needed.

Upon receiving client request R, the Matchmaker of B_K performs service composition. When needed, Matchmaker requests the Workload & Admission Control Predictor to make desired predictions. The service data stored in the Service Specification DB will be used for matchmaking and prediction (the specific method will be discussed in the later sections). After composing the concrete workflow $W = \{cs_1, cs_2, \ldots, cs_n\}$ for R, where cs_i is the concrete service as_i is grounded to, the Workflow Execution Manger of B_K manages the execution of W for the client. It monitors the execution status and maintains the execution state of cs_i, for all i, including the concrete services it does not host their information in its DB. In case a service is over time or the admission for a service request gets declined, B_K recomposes the remaining workflow in an attempt to avoid violating the service requirements of R.

4 Workload Prediction

We use ARIMA [13] as the basis for predicting the workload of the services. Time series can be stationary, or non-stationary. A time series is stationary when its statistical properties (e.g. mean, variance, covariance, correlation, etc.) are the same for all times. A non-stationary time series may have seasonality and/or trend and the differencing operator can be used to eliminate the trend and seasonality in them. Sometimes, we have to repeat the differencing process (higher order of differencing) for a time series till it becomes stationary. This is the way to find the order of seasonality and trend in a time series. Consider a time series z, the differenced operation can be written as $z_t' = z_t - z_{t-1}$, where z_t and z_{t-1} are the series value at time t and $t - 1$, respectively.

Stationary time series is one whose properties do not depend on the time at which the series is observed. For simplicity, we introduce the backward shift operator, B, where $Bz_t = z_{t-1}$. In general, a d-th order difference is $(1 - B)^d z_t$.

The seasonal ARIMA model incorporates both the non-seasonal and seasonal factors. Therefore, the seasonal ARIMA model can be denoted as $ARIMA(P, D, Q)(p, d, q)_m$ where p is the non-seasonal AR (Autoregressive model) order, d is the non-seasonal differencing, q is the non-seasonal MA (Moving Average model) order, P is the seasonal AR order, D is the seasonal differencing, Q is the seasonal MA order, and m is the time span of repeating the seasonal pattern. m is the number of periods per season.

In our approach, we focus on the seasonal ARIMA model. We provide its definition below without the derivation details.

$$\left(1 - \emptyset_1 B - \ldots - \emptyset_p B^p\right)\left(1 - \Phi_1 B^m - \ldots - \Phi_p B^{mP}\right) \times (1 - B)(1 - B^m)Z_t$$
$$= \left(1 - \theta_1 B - \ldots - \theta_q B^q\right) \times \left(1 - \Theta_1 B^m - \ldots - \Theta_q B^{mQ}\right) \times e_t$$

where e_t is the white noise (zero mean and constant variance), $\Phi_1, \Phi_2, \ldots, \Phi_p$ are the weight parameters for the Autoregressive of order P, $AR(p)$, part. The $\theta_1, \theta_2, \ldots, \theta_q$ are the weight parameters for the Moving Average of order q, $MA(q)$ part.

When using the ARIMA model, we need to select the parameters $p, d, q, P, D,$ and Q for the input time series, which is not an easy process. We use the ARIMA package in

R to make the selection of these parameters. The package also estimates the $\theta_i, \emptyset_i, \Theta_i, \Phi_i$ parameters as well.

The workloads of most web services have seasonality and trend. In our approach, we use the seasonal ARIMA model for analyzing and predicting service workloads.

5   Two-Phase Composition Algorithm

We predict workload and estimate the admission control outcome of the concrete service hosts to achieve service composition with lower risk of execution time failures. But this adds an overhead to the service composition time. To overcome this issue, we adopted a similar concept as in our previous work [17] and fit it in our prediction based service composition process. Let $\{cs_i^1, cs_i^2, \ldots, cs_i^{m_i}\}$ denote the m_i concrete services identified by the broker for grounding the abstract service as_i. The broker selects the final composition candidates using a two-phase composition algorithm. The candidate with the best QoS is selected for grounding and the broker monitors the service execution for recomposition in case of failure.

The cs shares its specifications with the brokers that subscribe it. It shares its QoS levels which is denoted as cs. $cs.Q = \langle TQ, q_1, \ldots, q_q \rangle$ in terms of the $q+1$ QoS attributes. Where $cs.TQ$ is a tuple $\langle mrti, tilog \rangle$, $cs.mrti$ is the most recent timing data for cs, $cs.tilog$ is the log of timing data for cs. Each timing data (for the most recent data entry and the entries in the log) includes the specification $\langle [ts, te], avgload, avgrt \rangle$, which records the average load and average response time in time interval $[ts, te]$.

The two phases of the composition are discussed in the following two subsections.

5.1   Phase 1: Composition Candidate Selection

In the first phase, the broker, upon receiving composition request R from the client, selects, based on genetic algorithm, the K top candidate compositions, i.e., candidate workflows, and passes the ranked list of the K candidates for R to the second phase. The timing behaviors of the candidate workflows are estimated coarsely. For each candidate service $cs_i^{j_i}$, we only consider its $cs_i^{j_i}.ert$ which is the expected response time that $cs_i^{j_i}$ shares with the broker, where $cs_i^{j_i}$ is the j's concrete web service that can instantiate abstract service as_i, where service $j_i \leq m_i$.

The concrete web services selected for the composition candidate may belong to different providers and may be geographically located far from each other. Therefore, there would be a communication latency among the web services. The communication latency calculation considers both the location of the concrete web services, and the size of the data exchanged. The concrete web service, cs, shares its output parameters with the broker. The $cs.Out$ is the set of output parameters of cs and their total size is denoted by $cs.Out.Size$. In [15, 16], experiments have been conducted and the results show that the following equation can serve as a good estimate of the communication latency between two services, $cs_i^{j_i}$ and $cs_k^{j_k}$, with geographical distance $dist(cs_i^{j_i}, cs_k^{j_k})$ and message size of $cs_i^{j_i}.Out.Size$ which is the size of the $cs_i^{j_i}$ service output, $cs_i^{j_i}.Out$:

$$Latency\left(cs_i^{j_i}, cs_k^{j_k}\right) = 0.2 * \left(cs_i^{j_i}.Out.Size\right)^{0.51} * \left[0.4 + 0.3 \times dist\left(cs_i^{j_i}, cs_k^{j_k}\right)^{0.735}\right]$$
$$+ \left[0.4 + 0.3 \times dist\left(cs_i^{j_i}, cs_k^{j_k}\right)^{0.735}\right] \tag{1}$$

Thus, a candidate workflow $cwf = \langle cs_1^{j_1}, cs_2^{j_2}, \ldots, cs_n^{j_n}\rangle$, $1 \leq j_i \leq m_i$, should satisfy the QoS requirements given in R as follows:

$$\sum_{i=1}^{n} cs_i^{j_i}.ert + \sum_{i=1}^{n} Latency\left(cs_i^{j_i}, cs_k^{j_k}\right) \leq R.QR.TR, \text{ and}$$
$$CFQ(q)_{i=1}^{n} cs_i^{j_i}.q_q \text{ satisfies } R.QR.qr_q \tag{2}$$

Here, $CFQ(q)$ denotes the quality composition function for the q-th quality attribute. In this paper, we only focus on timing property and will not consider the composition of other quality attributes.

The candidate workflows satisfying the above constraints are added to the candidate list and the list is ranked according to how well the constraints are satisfied (based on a utility functions). The top K candidates are then passed to the second phase.

5.2 Phase 2: Fine-Grained Timing Analysis for Composition Decision Making

When a concrete web service in one of the top K candidate workflows is invoked, its workload at the time may be very different from its current workload. Existing composition approaches do not consider this problem. Consider a candidate workflow $cwf = \langle cs_1^{j_1}, cs_2^{j_2}, \ldots, cs_n^{j_n}\rangle$. $cs_i^{j_i}$'s invocation time depends on the cumulative response time of $cs_1^{j_1}$ through $cs_{i-1}^{j_{i-1}}$ plus the service invocation starting time provided in the composition request, $R.st$. Thus, the workload estimation for each concrete service should be as accurate as possible to avoid cumulative errors.

In the second phase, we use ARIMA to predict the workload of each concrete service $cs_i^{j_i}$ based on its historical workload $cs_i^{j_i}.tilog$. Let $cs_i^{j_i}.p\lambda(t)$ denote the predicted workload for $cs_i^{j_i}$ at a future time t. The prediction of $cs_i^{j_i}.p\lambda$ should be made for $cs_i^{j_i}$'s invocation time. Let IT_i denote the service invocation time of $cs_i^{j_i}$ in the workflow cwf for composition request R. We predict $cs_i^{j_i}$'s workload $cs_i^{j_i}.p\lambda(IT_i)$. Based on $cs_i^{j_i}.p\lambda(IT_i)$ and $cs_i^{j_i}$'s service rate $cs_i^{j_i}.\mu$, we can compute $cs_i^{j_i}$'s predicted average response time $cs_i^{j_i}.prt(IT_i)$ as follows:

$$cs_i^{j_i}.prt(IT_i) = \frac{1}{cs_i^{j_i}.\mu - cs_i^{j_i}.p\lambda(IT_i)}, \text{ where } IT_i = R.st + \sum_{x=1}^{i-1} cs_x^{j_x}.prt(IT_x) \tag{3}$$

With the new response time predication, now we can refine the candidate workflow timing behavior analysis given in Eq. (2). We have the new predicted average response time for cwf as

$$prt(cwf) = \sum_{i=1}^{n} cs_i^{j_i}.prt(IT_i) + \sum_{i=1}^{n} Latency\left(cs_i^{j_i}, cs_k^{j_k}\right) \tag{4}$$

Again, we rank the candidate workflow cwf based on its $prt(cwf)$ as well as its other quality attributes. We build the top K' candidate workflows with $prt(cwf) \leq prt(wf)$ and $CFQ(q)_{i=1}^{n} cs_i^{j_i}.q_q$ satisfies $R.qr_q$.

5.3   Admission Control Consideration

Service providers incorporate admission control to protect their servers from being overloaded and maintain the service quality within the committed level to satisfy customers' requirements. When web services incorporate admission control, the broker would need to take it into consideration when selecting service compositions. At composition time, the Matchmaker requests the Workload & Admission Control Predictor to predict the workload for each composite service at the corresponding invocation time. If any service in the concrete composite workflow has a high chance of not getting admitted, the broker drops the corresponding composition candidates.

Each web service pushes its admission control policy $cs.adm$ to its subscribing brokers. The admission control policy is defined by the tuple $\langle maxload, thAdm \rangle$, where $cs.maxload$ specifies the server load capacity and $cs.thAdm$ is the threshold for admission to cs, i.e., cs's admission control algorithm will reject new requests when its load reaches $cs.thAdm \times cs.maxLoad$.

To illustrate the process, when the broker validates a composite service cs_i^j, it first calculates its estimated invocation time, IT_i, as shown in Eq. (3), and then the workload for the web service is predicted at time IT_i, as $cs_i^{j_i}.p\lambda(IT_i)$.

The Workload and Adm. Ctl. Predictor would perform the following validation:

If $cs_i^{j_i}.p\lambda(IT_i) < ((cs_i^j.maxload * cs_i^j.thAdm)/100) =>$ most probably cs_i^j would be able to handle the new request.

If $cs_i^{j_i}.p\lambda(IT_i) \geq ((cs_i^j.maxload * cs_i^j.thAdm)/100) =>$ most probably cs_i^j would not be able to handle the new request, therefore the broker drops any service composition candidate with this composite service.

5.4   Service Execution

In our approach, the second phase builds the top K' service composition candidates and grounds the candidate with best predicted QoS. During service execution, the broker monitors the execution of each service in the composite workflow. If the execution at web service $cs_i^{j_i}$ succeeded, the broker is notified, then the broker confirms the admission with the next composite service, $cs_{i+1}^{j_{i+1}}$; if admission request is granted, then the broker directs $cs_i^{j_i}$ to forward its output data to $cs_{i+1}^{j_{i+1}}$. If admission request is rejected, then the broker triggers the recomposition process using the top K' candidates list and the service execution is resumed at the replacement of $cs_{i+1}^{j_{i+1}}$.

6 Experiment Study

In the experimental system, we setup a single broker and define 60 abstract services, each as_i has m_i candidate concrete services, where m_i is randomly generated in the range of [8, 12]. A total of 615 concrete web services have been created. Clients service requests are generated continuously to the system. The broker makes QoS based selection decisions to find the best service compositions that satisfy the clients' requests.

We compare the two-phase prediction based composition (TPC) approach proposed in this paper with a conventional composition (CC) solution. CC simply uses the current load of cs, cs.mrti maintained by the broker updated every 5 min, to derive the average response time of the cs and uses it to select the best composition decisions (only one phase).

6.1 Web Service and Workflow Parameter Generation

For each concrete service cs, we generate cs.avgrt, cs.Loc, and cs.tilog. Each web service simulates an m/m/n queue with service rate generated randomly from two service time sets, [1, 5] min and [5, 10] min. All the web services that belong to the first half of the abstract services use the first service time range, and the second half use the second range. We repeated the experiments with another 3 different service time sets, [10, 20] min and [15, 25] min, [20, 30] min and [25, 35] min, and [30, 50] min and [40, 60] min. The location of a web service cs, cs.Loc, is generated by uniformly randomly selecting an earth coordinate. We use the workload generation method discussed in Sect. 6.2 to generate cs.tilog. The workload for each concrete service cs is created offline, including its historical workload and the workload for the duration of the experiment. The same workload profile is used for both CC and TPC approaches. We also repeated the experiment with the sharper changing load and the noisy load using the last set of service time set.

In this paper, we consider that all service providers implement admission control, however, each may have different load capacity and threshold. The admission control in concrete service cs keeps track of cs.mrti and if cs.mrti.avgload exceeds (cs.thAdm × cs.maxLoad), cs rejects any new service requests until some existing requests complete their services. cs.thAdm is configurable and is set to 85% in the experiments. cs.maxLoad and the number of servers for each web server are generated using the m/m/n queue model for each web service based on their corresponding average service time.

Service requests are generated randomly using the Poisson process with an inter-arrival rate of 500 requests per minute. For each service request R, the client generates the parameters for R. The workflow R.awf is generated randomly and sequentially selecting n different abstract services to form the service chain. The experiment is repeated for the following values of the workflow size n: 4, 6, 8, and 10. The timing requirement R.TR is generated by summing the average response times of the abstract services (average over the corresponding concrete services) together with an additional percentage of time. Specifically, we have

$$R.TR = \sum_{i=1}^{n} \frac{\sum_{j=1}^{m_i} cs_i^{j_i}.avgrt}{m_i} * (1 + addt)$$

where $cs_i^{j_i}$ are the concrete services that match $R.as_i$ and $addt$ is a percentage of the overall average of all the web services of the workflow and it is randomly generated in the range [0.3, 0.6]. This will allow randomness in the time requirements and creates the cases where not finding a service composition that meets the requirements easy, hard, and not possible. If service composition execution takes longer than this value, the request will be marked as failed with QoS violation.

We also consider the communication latency when estimating the service request arrival time and the overall workflow response time. The communication latency is calculated as per Eq. (1). A communication latency of x time units is simulated by holding the message sending activity for x time units.

6.2   Workload Generation Using Decompose

In order to evaluate our two-phase approach, we need to simulate the composition activities and generate workloads for each of the concrete web services. To make the generated loads as close to real world workloads as possible, we first analyze the workloads of real servers and extract important parameters from them.

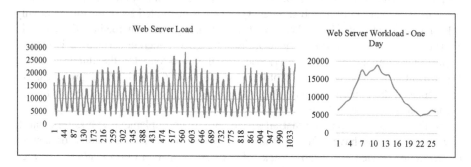

Fig. 2. Generated workload

We analyze the workload data extracted from real services provided in [14]. These workload data are decomposed using the decompose() function provided in R into the trend, seasonal, and irregular components. The parameters for the three components are analyzed and adjusted to generate new workloads for web services. Based on the workload analysis and generation scheme, we generate simulated workload. Figure 2 shows a sample workload we generated for the duration of a few weeks. It shows the weekly as well as daily seasonality. It also shows the lower workloads on weekends compared to those of weekdays. Figure 2 also zooms in to show a closer look of the data over one day. It shows that the load started very low after midnight and started to climb in the morning to get the peak time and then started to go down again in the afternoon and evening time.

6.3   Simulated Workflow Execution

The broker processes a composition request R and outputs the concrete workflow $R.wf$. Assume that the abstract service in wf, $R.as_1, R.as_2, \ldots, R.as_n$, are grounded to $cs_1^{j_1}$, $cs_2^{j_2}$, $\ldots$, $cs_n^{j_n}$. We execute R by sending a message to $cs_1^{j_1}$ at the workflow starting time $R.st$. If $cs_1^{j_1}$ is overloaded and its admission control mechanism decides to deny R, $cs_1^{j_1}$ immediately responds back that the invocation has failed. Otherwise, $cs_1^{j_1}$ computes the estimated expected response time ert for R based on its current workload using m/m/n queuing theory, waits for ert time units, and then invokes $cs_2^{j_2}$ to continue the execution.

During the execution of wf, if at least one concrete web service has rejected R, then the broker will be notified. In this case if the request deadline is reached, the request is marked as failed, otherwise a re-composition is triggered for un-executed composite services. If the execution succeeds, then we record the event as successful together with the response time of executing wf.

In the experiments, we use a scale for the time so the real 1 min is one testing hour, otherwise executing each experiment would take a very long time. The broker plays a central role to synchronize the time by setting the testing start time and broadcasting it to all nodes using a time synchronization message.

Each simulated system runs for 10 weeks (in simulated time). We measure the request success rates and the response time of the composition and execution phases and compare CC and TPC algorithms with different service time sets, workflow sizes, and with/without admission control. We repeat the test with different workload profiles and evaluate the impact of workload patterns on the approaches.

7   Experimental Results

Figure 3 shows the success rate for CC and TPC with different service time and workflow size settings. It shows clearly that TPC outperform the CC approach in all scenarios. With the first service time set (overall average of 5 min), TPC performs between 4.4% to 14.2% better than CC depending on the workflow size. When the workflow size increases, the advantage of TPC increases. Similarly, when the we used the higher service time set, TPC advantage becomes bigger. For example, when we use the last service time set (overall average 45 min), the TPC advantage over CC is between 10.2% and 34.9%. When we used the first service time set, CC performance is closer to TPC especially when using workflow size 4 since with CC approach the broker is receiving the current load for the web services every 5 min, so with service time 1, CC decision is better. CC performance declines when workflow size increases because now it needs to plan composition with longer time ahead. When planning for long time ahead, using work load prediction shows much better performance.

For the experiments, we look closer to the prediction performance by looking into the number of times we had web service admission control rejecting the service request due to a bad decision by Workload and Adm. Ctl. (admission control) Predictor of the broker when building the service composition. Figure 3 above also shows the broker decision performance for different experiment settings (e.g. workflow size, service time) for both CC and TPC approaches.

The graph shows a big advantage of using the TPC approach over the CC approach. Using the prediction based approach, the broker is able to make the right decision when building composition and the success rate is between 93% when workflow size is 4 and 83% when workflow size is 10 when using the first service time set. When comparing this to CC performance using the same experiment setting, the broker was able to make the right decision between 82% and 62%. When using other service time sets, the TPC performance is almost the same with slight degradation. However, the CC performance degrades significantly. The significance of the broker making the right decision is not only to find a reliable service composition but also faster by eliminating the re-composition requirement possibility and therefore meeting the client's deadline requirement.

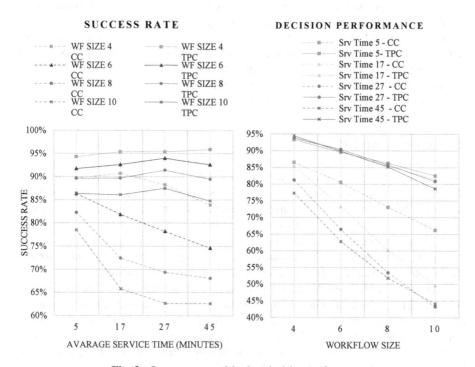

Fig. 3. Success rate and broker decision performance

To evaluate the admission control impact, we turned off admission control and repeated the experiment for different service time sets with workflow set to 6 in all cases and for both approaches CC and TPC. Figure 4 below shows the comparison for the same scenarios with admission control turned on.

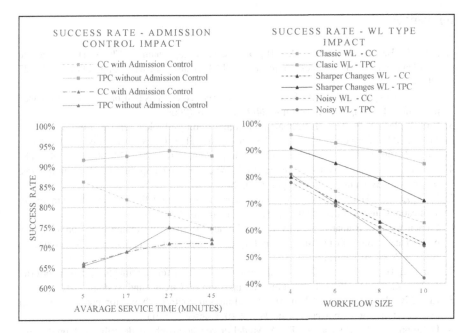

Fig. 4. Admission control impact and workload type impact

The graph shows the bad performance when web services don't implement admission control. This is clearly due to the relatively very high response time by web services that are running high load and keep accepting new requests. This will cause the service request to miss the deadline set by the client when the request is initiated.

The first workload profile we used for the experiment was the typical web service workload profile which is low during night and high during the day. We repeated the experiment with another two different workload profiles, one with sharper changes to the load, and the other with noisier workload. Figure 4 shows also the performance of the CC and TPC approaches using the three workload profiles.

Both CC and TPC degrade significantly with noisy load. This is expected for TPC since prediction becomes less accurate with about 40% prediction errors. For the case of sharper workload changes, the prediction error is around 20%. Also, CC gets less advantage with the 5-min load information updates when the load is noisy or when the workload changes faster.

8 Conclusion

We have proposed a service performance management framework which uses workload prediction to enable more accurate service time analysis in order to achieve better service composition with lower risk of execution time failures due to insufficient timing analysis. Though timing failures still may occur and continuous monitoring and dynamic recomposition are still incorporated in the framework, the experimental results show that the risk of incurring such timing failures is greatly reduced.

References

1. Zeng, L., Benatallah, B., Ngu, A.H.H., Dumas, M., Kalagnanam, J., Chang, H.: QoS-aware middleware for web services composition. IEEE Trans. Software Eng. **30**(5), 311–327 (2004)
2. Dai, Y., Yang, L., Zhang, B.: Self-healing web service composition based on performance prediction. J. Comput. Sci. Technol. **24**(2), 250–261 (2009)
3. Yan, Y., Poizat, P., Zhao, L.: Repair vs. recomposition for broken service compositions. In: Maglio, P.P., Weske, M., Yang, J., Fantinato, M. (eds.) ICSOC 2010. LNCS, vol. 6470, pp. 152–166. Springer, Heidelberg (2010). https://doi.org/10.1007/978-3-642-17358-5_11
4. Ma, H., Bastani, F., Yen, I.-L., Mei, H.: QoS-driven service composition with reconfigurable services. IEEE Trans. Serv. Comput. **6**(1), 20–34 (2011)
5. Bi, J., Zhu, Z., Tian, R., Wang, Q.: Dynamic provisioning modeling for virtualized multi-tier applications in cloud data center. In: IEEE Cloud (2010)
6. Calheiros, R.N., Ranjany, R., Buyya, R.: Virtual machine provisioning based on analytical performance and QoS in cloud computing environments. In: International Conference on Parallel Processing (2011)
7. Nan, X., He, Y., Guan, L.: Optimal resource allocation for multimedia cloud in priority service scheme. In: IEEE International Symposium on Circuits and Systems (2012)
8. Chen, X., Mohapatra, P., Chen, H.: An admission control scheme for predictable server response time for Web accesses. In: WWW10. Citeseer (2001)
9. D'Ambrogio, A., Bocciarelli, P.: A Model-driven approach to describe and predict the performance of composite services. In: WOSP (2007)
10. Van Hoecke, S., Verdickt, T., Dhoedt, B., Gielen, F., Demeester, P.: Modelling the performance of the Web Service platform using layered queueing networks. In: SAVCBS (2005)
11. Wu, Q., Zhang, M., Zheng, R., Lou, Y., Wei, W.: A QoS-satisfied prediction model for cloud-service composition based on a hidden markov model. Math. Probl. Eng. Article ID 387083, 7 p. (2013)
12. Ye, Z., Mistry, S., Bouguettaya, A.: Long-term-aware cloud service composition using multivariate time series analysis. IEEE Trans. Serv. Comput. **9**(3), 382–393 (2016)
13. Hyndman, R.J., Athanasopoulos, G.: Forecasting, Principles and Practice, 2nd edn. Otexts, Melbourne (2018)
14. Reiss, C., Wilkes, J., Hellerstein, J.: Google, 17 November 2014. https://drive.google.com/file/d/0B5g07T_gRDg9Z0lsSTEtTWtpOW8/view. Accessed 2016
15. Ye, Y., Yen, I.-L., Xiao, L., Thuraisingham, B.: Secure, highly available, and high performance peer-to-peer storage systems. In: IEEE (2008)
16. Zhang, H., Goel, A., Govindan, R.: An empirical evaluation of internet latency expansion. ACM SIGCOMM Comput. Commun. Rev. **35**(1), 93–97 (2005)
17. Moussa, H., Gao, T., Yen, I.-L., Bastani, F., Jeng, J.-J.: Toward effective service composition for real-time SOA-based systems. SOCA **4**, 17–31 (2010)

Chatbot Assisted Marketing in Financial Service Industry

Jon T. S. Quah[(✉)] and Y. W. Chua

Singapore Institute of Management,
461 Clementi Road, Singapore 599491, Singapore
jonquah@sim.edu.sg

Abstract. The rise of chatbots in the finance sector is the latest disruptive force that has change the way customers interact. The adoption of Artificial Intelligence powered chatbots particularly in the banking industry has changed the face of communication interface between bank and customers. This paper explores the effectiveness of the current use of chatbot in Singapore's banking industry. The banking sector in Singapore play a significant role in Singapore economy. It also investigates the current chatbot functionality to determine if it can meet the ever-changing expectation of customers.

Keywords: Chatbot · Fintech · User-profiling · Service level

1 Introduction

Chatbots, fueled by artificial intelligence, have been identify as a need for business as it is able to provide immediate communication with customers at anytime and anywhere. Chatbot is identify as one of the key success factor to business success which banks in the financial industry are adopting. Chatbot is an artificial intelligence robot that imitates human conversation through commands, text chat, or both. It's a virtual conversation in which the customers communicate with an online talking robot. Chatbots are currently operating in various channels which include web and messaging platform. For example, Mastercard utilize chatbot on Facebook Messenger to provide better digital services where customers, can reap the benefit of the bots to help review their purchase history, spending habits, and account balance.

Banks especially in the developed countries such as Singapore are leveraging on artificial intelligence in their digital strategy. However, despite being ranked one of the most digital savvy countries, Singaporean are still conservative in natural. They are also resistance to change and prefer traditional methods. Through this research, we investigate the receptiveness of Singaporean towards chatbot implemented by the banks.

2 Adoption of A.I. by Financial Service Industry

Fintech is a new financial industry that applies technology to improve financial activities (Schueffel 2016). Artificial Intelligence has resulted in new technologies coming into play which have an impact on human live. In recent years, there is an

J. E. Ferreira et al. (Eds.): SCC 2019, LNCS 11515, pp. 107–114, 2019.
https://doi.org/10.1007/978-3-030-23554-3_8

increase in fintech startups, company that leverage on AI to create better quality financial services. Large financial institutions are beginning to partner and invest with fintechs to gain competitive advantage over traditional banks as well as to ensure digital advancement. Chatbot is a conversational agent that mimic interaction with real people. The most advance chatbot systems can employ machine learning to adapt new information or user requests. Chatbot are typically found in messaging applications such as Facebook messenger (since 2016), WhatsApp, WeChat (since 2013) or via SMS. Today, these chatbots are used for B2C sales, customer service and marketing.

After the 2008 financial crisis, it had led to a profound economic implication for the banks. Profit margins have declined for the banks over the last decade. Therefore, banks try to improve on the internal operational efficiency and reduce cost of customer support to maintain profitability even in the event of future financial crisis. Chatbot technologies is able to handle voluminous calls from customer and increase satisfaction while changing the customers' opinion of the bank. As tech giants such as Alibaba and Amazon are setting a higher bar for customer expectation, banks need to be able to harness and improve the ability of conversational AI-backed platform to cater to the need of the banking customers.

3   Objective and Research Methods

The objectives of this project and the different methodologies to achieve the stated objectives will be described below. The chosen methods used in this study are analyzed and justified.

3.1   Objective of the Project

The objectives are:

1. The current customer experience of chatbot used by the bank
2. What factors affect the adoption of chatbot in Singapore

3.2   Methodology

A few methods were used to achieve the objectives stated above:

1. Studying and analyzing the past related research
2. Conducting interview to gather further insights

3.2.1   Study Past Related Research

Due to the non-disclosure policy of the banks, there is limited published study on chatbot usage by the banks. We will study general literature on chatbot usage and use it as reference to measure the effectiveness and satisfaction of the chatbots usage by banks in Singapore. This is followed by an in-depth study of which main group of users would prefer the use of chatbot and if it provide them with the result they want to achieve.

3.2.2   Interview

For this research, a mixed methodology was used. Face to face interviews were conducted over a few weeks. During the interview, qualitative user tests were conducted.

The reason interview was chosen as a method was because the interviews can provide qualitative input for rich and contextual exploration of the chatbot. Furthermore, the interviewees are required to use the bank Virtual Assistant chatbot to perform certain bank services during the interview. The Virtual Assistant chatbot was chosen as it's the only chatbot in Singapore bank that provide general customer services.

The data collected enabled statistical analysis on the expectation and customer experience of the chatbots. This will provide better understanding of current implementation of chatbot technology by the banks and compare determine whether the current chatbot meet the expectation of the interviewees. This will identify the strength and weakness of current chatbot and suggest improvement to increase adoption of chatbot technology.

A set of metrics were used to measure the expectation and customer experience of the chatbot. User experience will measure the response rate, functionality and usability. Response rate measure how fast the chatbot reply to an enquiry. Functionality measured if the chatbot can understand the enquiry asked by the user and follow up with proper answer. It also measured the accuracy of the speech synthesis. Usability refer to how easy is it to use the chatbot. This is important especially for non-tech savvy users. If the chatbot is not easy to use, users will likely not use it the next time.

To measure satisfaction, the metrics used were interactivity, informative, data privacy and protection. Interactivity include greeting the user as well as providing emotional information through tone, inflection and expressivity. This is to make the conversation more fun and interesting. It enables user to feel like they are interacting with human. Informative refer to how detailed the information provided by the chatbot is. Data privacy and protection refer to how secure is the chatbot in term of protecting the personal details while the user is conversing with the chatbot.

This study provides a gauge of the user adoption of chatbot in Singapore. It also identifies which factor affect the overall usage of the chatbot. The analysis will provide insights if chatbot can provide better value-added services than bank staffs so as to determine the extent in which the bank can replace existing staffs to reduce cost.

4   Discussion and Argument

Quality attributes of chatbots are breakdown into 3 different categories. The effectiveness, efficiency and satisfaction with which specified users achieve specified goals into particular environments (Shawar 2007). Efficiency implies to how well the resources are allocated to achieve certain goals. According to Oliver (1997), satisfaction is a pleasurable fulfilment. In general, consumers complete some goals and desire. Consequently, this completion creates a pleasurable feeling. Quality attributes are subjective. Most researchers feel chatbot or conversational agent should priorities interreacting and responding like a human, others such as Wilson (2017) think otherwise. The common ground is chatbots must boost users' experience to be considered successful.

According to a survey by HSBC (2017) 66% of Singaporean currently use online banking but only 9% of Singaporean adventure into banking apps via smart phone to manage money. The study shows that although Singaporean are tech-literate, the lack of knowledge to combat cyber risks has result in the low confident level to uptake new technologies by the banks. The banks have taken measure to address this issue by implementing security features to build up the customers confident in new techonologies, such as fingerprint recognition and one-time password. The Monetary Authority of Singapore (MAS) has also impose stricter regulations such as Personal Data Protection Act (PDPA) on the banks. Such measure helps to protect the customers from potential banking system vulnerabilities.

4.1   Banking Chatbots in Singapore

In Singapore, a wealthy nation with high computer literacy, 79% of the interviewees are willing to use computer-generated support for business services and purchase of bank products. To remain competitive, banks will have to adapt their traditional services by implementing robotics into their banking services that will enable the banks to capture more market share.

Industry	Percentage (%):
IT	15
Finance	31
Airline	2
Government	4
Human Resource	3
Logistic	4
Maritime	3
Marketing	6
Telecom	1
Medical	2
Student	26
Transport	2
Bakery	1

Fig. 1. Breakdown of interviewees working in different industries who uses banking chatbots

Figure 1 shows the breakdown in percentage of interviewees of our study who use chatbots according to the industries they are working in. It is noted that 46% of interviewees who use chatbots are either in IT industry or finance industry. Another 26% are students who, in Singapore, have IT exposure at a young age. The use of IT in the Singapore education system plays a part in the high IT literacy rate in Singapore.

These three groups of chatbots users add up to 72% of those who have such experience. It can be expected that acceptance of chatbots technology will likely follow similar diffusion path like that of Internet banking in the 2000s.

At a prominent major bank in Singapore, chatbots are able to handle over 82% of requests without any human intervention. Furthermore, it only requires 20% of the resources of a traditional bank. As such, the bank is planning to roll out its chatbot service to other mobile messaging apps such as Whatsapp and WeChat. The bank also plans to increase its services which allow the chatbot to advise on customers with regards to purchase of bank products such as investment or insurance. In order for banks to roll out its chatbot service to other platform, it must be able to provide positive user experience.

A recent study by Singapore Institute of Management on Chatbot users yield the following results (Fig. 2):

Criteria of chatbot (1 being least important and 6 being most important)	Rank 1	Rank 2	Rank 3	Rank 4	Rank 5	Rank 6	Total Score
Interactivity	38	4	17	15	26	0	285
Informative	0	0	19	0	8	73	537
Data Privacy and Protection	48	26	0	7	4	15	214
Fast Respone	0	4	0	30	55	11	467
Functionality	0	36	12	48	4	0	286
Easy To Use	15	29	52	0	4	0	222

Fig. 2. Desired features of chatbots

The result showed that informative information by the chatbot are rated the highest priority. This is followed by fast response, functionality, interactivity, easy to use and data privacy and protection.

Most of the interviewees ranked informative as the top criteria are well-educated with diploma and above. On the other hand, data privacy and protection was the least priority. From the Norton cybersecurity insight report, 37% of the Millennials do not think they will become a target even though 52% of them had experienced cybercrime. This indicate that millennials are complacent about online security and not adopting safe cyber habits. Therefore, banks must have high security features put in place to ensure that information within the chatbot services are kept privacy and confidential. A breach in the security of the chatbot services may result in confident level of customers adopting the use of chatbot.

For the group that seeks convenience as the top priority, most interviewees find that as long as chatbot is convenience and positive user experience, they will continue to use the chatbot.

At the other end of the continuum, 6% of the interviewees which are not part of the millennials indicate that they would not use chatbot. They prefer the human touch of going through banks staff and 40% of them do not have access to the technology to use the chatbot. Unless the chatbot is able to reproduce the same human touch as the bank staff, it will be difficult for this group of people to adopt to the chatbot technology. As a result, it will be hard for banks to move all its services and operations to the chatbot platform. Banks may have to invest more money and resources to train this group of customers to be competence to use the chatbot technology.

4.2 Customer Experience of Chatbot in Singapore

Base on the study of the interview, it was found that there was a direct link between how informative the chatbot is and customer experience. From the study, it was found out that 76% of the interviewees were not satisfied with the bank chatbot technology. The main reason for the negative customer experience was that the bank chatbot is not about to provide an immediate answer that the customers need when they use it. This group of interviewees search for information on the interest rate of the house loan, current bank interest rate in saving account as well as investment funds performance to make a comparison between other banks make better decision. The current chatbot technology is only about to track the keyword provided by the customer and provide them with the most suitable link. Even though the chatbot is able to reply immediately and easy to use, the criteria on being informative still outranked the rest. This resulted in overall negative customer experience. This group of interviewees belong to the millennial group and will not continue to use it nor introduce to their friends or family. How fast and relevant is chatbot is able provide the customers with the information will affect the rate of adoption of chatbot technology in the banking sector in Singapore especially for the millennial.

A small percentage of the interviewees who are not satisfy with the bank chatbot are not part of the millennial. They belong to the aging population category. The reason why they are not satisfy with chatbot is because some of them are not IT savvy enough to use the chatbot while the rest are resistance to change. This group of interviewees prefer the traditional ways to enquire information which is to go down to the bank directly to enquire. This is a habit which is hard to break. In addition, this group of interviewees have low confident with data privacy and protection with using bank chatbot with fear that the information will be leaked out.

24% of interviewees that are satisfy with bank chatbot are those that did not rank informative as the top criteria they expect from bank chatbot. This group of people are not the millennial and most of them ranked convenience as their top criteria. They ask general information such as location of nearest bank or the opening hour for the bank which the chatbot can immediately provide answer with the right link. As such, this group of interviewees had a positive experience with bank chatbot and will continue to use it in the future.

4.3 Going Forward

Most survey interviewees feel chatbot need to be able to interpret and understand the questions by the users better. Furthermore, tacit knowledge of banks must be incorporated into the knowledge base. Before that is achieved, chatbots and human tellers will have to teamed up to serve the customers.

5 Conclusion

As the banks progress towards digital savvy entitles, many have found success in introducing IT by offering user-friendly features. In order to remain competitive, financial institution have to adapt their traditional services by introducing automation to attract increasingly tech-savvy customers. Moving forward, chatbots are posed to provide more than just automated savings. It is envisaged they will enter into wealth management for the masses with considerations of individual customer's risk profile, underwrite loans and insurance, provide data analyses and advanced analytics, and detect and notify of fraudulent behavior, all through an automated virtual assistant.

Chatbot Technology enables banking services to be available at any place and any hour of the day. This reduces the operation costs for the banks significantly. For now, their implementation have not reach the maturity stage where it can handle complex banking services. There are rooms for improvement in term of interpreting customers questions and providing correct information that the customers seek. This will enhance customer experience where quality of information is the top criteria that customers seek when using the chatbot.

References

Khanna, A., Pandey, B., Vashishta, K., Kalia, K., Pradeepkumar, B., Das, T.: A study of today's A.I. through chatbots and rediscovery of machine intelligence. Int. J. u- e- Serv. Sci. Technol. **8**(7), 277–284 (2015)

Radziwill, N.M., Benton, M.C.: Evaluating quality of chatbots and intelligent conversational agents, pp. 1–21 (2017)

Shawar, B.A.: Different measurements metrics to evaluate a chatbot system. Association for Computational Linguistics, pp. 89–96 (2007)

Kuligowska, K.: Commercial chatbot: performance evaluation, usability metrics and quality standards of embodied conversational agents. Prof. Center Bus. Res. **2**, 1–16 (2015)

Schueffel, P.: Taming the best: a scientific definition of fintech. J. Innov. Manag. **4**(4), 32–54 (2016)

Tacadena, K.G.: The chatbot will see you now: Singapore banks turn to bots (2017). http://sbr.com.sg/financial-services/in-focus/chatbot-will-see-you-now-singapore-banks-turn-%E2%80%98bots. Accessed 3 Nov 2017

Morgan, B.: 5 ways chatbots can improve customer experience in banking (2017). https://www.forbes.com/sites/blakemorgan/2017/08/06/5-ways-chatbots-can-improve-customer-experience-in-banking/#245c9c4a7148. Accessed 3 Nov 2017

Walker, J.: Chatbots to improve customer experience at banks (2017). http://www.digitaljournal.com/tech-and-science/technology/chatbots-to-improve-the-customer-experience-at-banks/article/504780. Accessed 3 Nov 2017

DBS Group Holding Ltd. Annual Report 2016, 2017: Reimagine Banking World's Best Digital Bank. https://www.dbs.com/annualreports/2016/english/pdf/01_DBS%20Annual%20Report%202016-Full.pdf. Accessed 10 Dec 2017

Tham, I.: DBS rolls out chatbot on Facebook messenger for online banking (2017). http://www.straitstimes.com/tech/dbs-rolls-out-chatbot-on-facebook-messenger-for-online-banking. Accessed 10 Dec 2017

Marketing Interactive: DBS launches innovative digital banking mobile app (2016). http://www.marketing-interactive.com/dbs-launches-digital-banking-mobile-app-dbs-digibank/. Accessed 10 Dec 2017

Singapore Business Review: Rise of the chatbots: here's how Singapore's big banks are adopting fintech (2017). http://sbr.com.sg/financial-services/in-focus/rise-chatbots-heres-how-singapores-big-banks-are-adopting-fintech. Accessed 2 Feb 2018

Yong, C.S.: Digital natives, much? Millennials are not as cyber-safe as they are cyber-savvy, e27 (2017). https://e27.co/digital-natives-much-millennials-not-cyber-safe-cyber-savvy-20170217/. Accessed 5 Feb 2018

Norton: Norton cybersecurity insights report (2017). https://sg.norton.com/cyber-security-insights. Accessed 13 Feb 2018

HSBC: Trust in technology (2017). http://www.hsbc.com/trust-in-technology-report. Accessed 2 Feb 2018

Oliver, R.L.: Satisfaction: A Behavioral Perspective on the Consumer. McGraw-Hill (1997)

Wilson, Y.C.T.: Seminar 'Development of Chatbot Technologies and Challenges'. Center for Data Science and Analytics (2017)

Application of Deep Learning in Surface Defect Inspection of Ring Magnets

Xu Wang[✉] and Pan Cheng

Sankyo Precision (Huizhou) Co., Ltd, Huizhou, China
wdx04@outlook.com

Abstract. We present a method of inspecting surface defects of ring magnets by using deep learning technology, and the inspection system developed utilizing this method has achieved much better accuracy and speed than human inspectors in actual production environment, while such accuracy and speed are essential for such systems. The proposed method can also be used for the surface defect inspection of many other industrial products and systems.

Keywords: Machine vision · Defect inspection · Image processing · Deep learning · Semantic segmentation · Caffe · Global convolution network

1 Introduction

Ring magnet is a kind of permanent magnet with strong magnetism, and it is one of the core components of magnetron. The quality of ring magnets has a decisive impact on the quality and service life of microwave ovens.

The commonly used ring magnets has thickness between the 11 mm–13 mm, the outer diameter between the 50–67 mm. There are more than 10 types of magnet surface defects, including (long) cracks, short cracks, circular cracks, hard material, impurities, broken edges, residual magnetism, broken or uneven chamfer, non-polished edges, sand eyes, soldering, etc., but can be summed up as two large categories - linear defects and blob defects. Among all the defects, short cracks are short linear defects usually appear at the edge of the inner ring of magnets, which needs to be detected at a resolution of 0.04 mm/pixel, while other defects can be detected at a lower resolution of the 0.10 mm/pixel. For each ring magnet we need to inspect both the front side and the back side, and magnet manufacturers require machine vision inspection systems to match the speed of the production line, which is around 120–140 pcs per minute.

At present, ring magnets manufacturers generally use a large number of inspectors to detect surface defects. For example, in our traditional factory setting, each production line needs to be equipped with at least 4 inspectors, naturally incurring high costs with high labor intensity, that eventually might fail to detect some defective products due to human visual fatigue.

The recent advances in applying artificial intelligence techniques in manufacturing systems has prompted us to explore the use of automated machine vision inspection instead of manual inspection in such systems. Before the advent of deep learning technology, the machine visual inspection industry detects product surface defects

© Springer Nature Switzerland AG 2019
J. E. Ferreira et al. (Eds.): SCC 2019, LNCS 11515, pp. 115–122, 2019.
https://doi.org/10.1007/978-3-030-23554-3_9

mainly by direct grayscale comparison or feature classification methods. Among them, the grayscale comparison method is to align the product image with a standard sample image, and then compare them pixel by pixel, judging by the grayscale difference. The disadvantage of this method is that it can only be used for products with very consistent appearances, such as printing labels, and can not be used with those with inconsistent appearances such as ring magnets. The method based on feature classification needs to extract image features using specially designed feature extractors (such as local binary pattern variants [1], HOG features [2], GLCM [3] and Gabor filters [4], etc.), and then use the extracted feature to train a classifier. The disadvantage of such an approach is that it is often difficult to design a good feature extractor, while only the classifier can be improved by training, the feature extractor itself cannot be trained, thus limiting the quality of the extracted features. Due to those problems with the traditional methods, many scientific institutions and machine vision companies had tried to develop a magnet surface defect inspection system, but all failed because their failure rate and false alarm rate can not be lowered to the acceptable range. Deep learning fuses the feature extractor and classifier into one integrated neural network, thus resolves the problem that the feature extractor cannot be trained, and at the same time, the deep neural networks with convolution structures have demonstrated with much better results than the traditional methods in many computer vision challenges such as ImageNet [5] and Pascal VOC [6]. So we believe that deep learning can solve the problem of feature extraction and enable us to develop a fully automated ring magnet surface defect inspection system to help our customers reduce production costs and improve product quality.

2   General Architecture

The general process of applying deep learning technology in machine vision systems is divided into two phases: training and prediction. The process of the training phase is as follows:

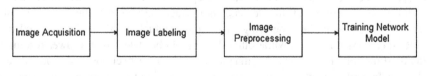

The process of prediction is as follows:

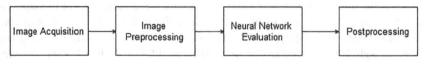

The first step in both phases is to acquire the product images. In the training stage, after the image is acquired, it is necessary to manually label the defects in the image, and then randomly produce a series of training samples (image-label pairs) of the same size through a pre-processing program, feed into the deep learning software for training, and finally obtain the parameter values of the neural network. During the prediction phase, some simple pre-processing is also required after the image has been acquired, mainly by scaling and cutting the image into several small batches, each of which is the same size as the images used for training, and then the batches are fed into the neural network for prediction. In the post-processing step, we stitch each part of the prediction result back into a complete image, then analyze the connected components in the image, calculate the size of each defect component, compare it with the user's preset allowable size, to determine whether the product is OK.

3 Image Acquisition

In machine vision systems, in order to acquire clear images over a short exposure time, high-brightness LED lights are usually used to light the target product. In practice, we use a high-angle ring light to acquire a bright-field image, which has high overall brightness that can clearly reflect the product surface details, and suitable for detecting most types of the surface defects such as long cracks and soldering, but the brightness of the chamfer part is low, and it is also difficult to detect short cracks. To complement that, we also use a low-angle ring light to acquire a dark-field image at the same place, which can clearly show the chamfer, suitable for checking chamfer integrity and detecting short cracks. Then we synthesize both images to create a pseudo-color RGB image to increase the amount of information provided to the neural network, in which Green = Bright-field image, Blue = Dark-field image, Red = Green-Blue. The original resolution of the image is 2048 × 2048 pixels, but most defects (defects other than short cracks) can be detected under lower resolutions, so we resize the image to 640 × 640 pixels for further processing (Figs. 1 and 2).

Fig. 1. Image acquisition hardware placement. From the top down: the grayscale camera, the high angle ring light, the low angle ring light (Color figure online)

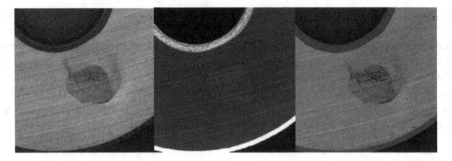

Fig. 2. Bright-field image, Dark-field image and the synthesized image (Color figure online)

4 Labeling of Images

To train a supervised neural network model, we need to label the acquired images to provide supervision information to the training process. We mark the linear defects with red lines and use blue brushes to mark the contours of blob defects. In addition, for dirty parts on the product surface that should not be considered as a defect, we use a white brush to mark its outline and ignore it during training. We did not apply different markers for each defect type, so the trained deep network can not output the precise defect type. But it is not an issue here, because all defect types in the blob category have similar allowable sizes, and it is almost the same for linear category defects, except for short cracks. Also, it is possible to recover part of the defect type information during post-processing, using the position/shape/line direction information of the defect (Fig. 3).

Fig. 3. Labeled defective images: long crack, hard material, soldering

5 Image Pre-processing

We have collected images from 1900 defective products and about 400 good products, for a total of 2322 images, of which 2100 are used for training and the rest are used for validation. Due to the complexity and varied size of defects and the limited number of labeled images, we have written a pre-processing program to augment the labeled images using a variety of transformations, including: random brightness changes, random scaling, random rotation, random cropping. The pre-processing program can produce over 400,000 pairs of 256 × 256 training samples. In practice, we actually trained three neural networks, one to detect general defects, one specifically to detect short cracks and one to detect chamfer defects, all three neural networks have similar structure, only differs in the number of down-sampling blocks. And the image resolution used by the latter two is reduced to 64 × 64 and 128 × 128 respectively, Only the largest 256 × 256 neural networks used to detect most defect types are discussed below.

6   The Neural Network Model

The purpose of surface defect detection is to find out the defective part of the product, from the point of view of image processing, we may treat a defect as an "object" or as a "region" in the image. Considering that in actual production we often need to obtain accurate contours of defects to calculate their length or area, rather than just a bounding box, we prefer to treat a defect as a region, that is, to segment the entire image into a number of normal regions and different categories of defective regions, which is a kind of semantic image segmentation task. In recent years, the neural network architecture proposed for semantic image segmentation includes Fully Convolutional Network FCN [7], SegNet [8], DeepLab series [9], Global convolution network GCN [10], ExFuse [11] and so on. Among them, DeepLab and GCN expand the effective receptive field of neurons through dilated convolution and separable convolution respectively, both achieved high segmentation accuracy. Considering that dilated convolution is harder to optimize with current computing hardware and is slower than separable convolution when the accuracy is similar, we actually adopt the neural network model based on GCN and add the SEB structure introduced in ExFuse. Each Res-x layer contains two modified ResNet blocks, each of which uses a structure similar to the GCN block, which uses two sets of 5 × 1 and 1 × 5 convolution and 1 × 1 convolution layers instead of stacked 3 × 3 convolution layers in the original ResNet, while the GCN block uses two sets of 7 × 1 and 1 × 7 convolution layers. We also changed the structure of each down-sampling block according to [12]. The neural network outputs 4 channels of the same width and height as the input image, channel 0 is the classification probability of background, channel 1 is the classification probability linear defect the channel 2 is the classification probability of blob defect, and channel 3 is for the ignored regions (Fig. 4).

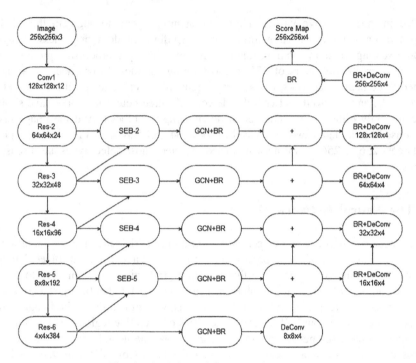

Fig. 4. Overview of the network structure

7   Training Procedure and Results

We use Caffe to train the above neural network model. Since defective pixels account for a small part of the entire image, we use a modified SoftmaxWithLoss layer which supports class weighting as the Loss layer of our neural network model, to accelerate learning from imbalanced data, and we set the weight of the harder-to-learn linear defects to 3.75, and weight of blob defect to 1.5. We use the Nesterov solver with momentum, the batch size is set to 32, the initial learning rate is 2.0e–4. Every 5000 iteration the learning rate is reduced to 0.8 times the previous one, and the weight decay is set to 5.0e–4, the momentum is set to 0.99. We count 5 epochs as a cycle, we re-generate all training samples after each cycle, and reset the learning rate to half of the initial learning rate of the previous cycle. We trained the model for a total of 12 cycles.

Considering the accuracy of manual labeling of images and the characteristics of defect detection tasks, we have loosened the calculation of IoU and recall rates, when the predicted defect mask is wider than the label, but the difference is within 2 pixels, it will not hurt the IoU:

Relaxed IoU $= |\text{dilate}(\text{prediction} \cap \text{label}, 5 \times 5 \text{ disc}) \cap (\text{prediction} \cup \text{label})|/|\text{prediction} \cup \text{label}|$

Relaxed Recall $= |\text{dilate}(\text{predition}, 5 \times 5 \text{ disc}) \cap \text{label}|/|\text{label}|$

The following are the validation results, it can be seen that our model has a good recognition accuracy for both types of defects, increasing the network width can greatly improve the recognition accuracy of blob defects, but the impact on linear defects is less (Table 1).

Table 1. Validation results of the trained network model.

Convolution layers	109	109
Conv1 output channels	12	16
Parameters	2.2 M	3.9 M
Pixel Accuracy	99.81%	99.83%
mean Relaxed IoU (linear defects)	82.12%	83.14%
mean Relaxed IoU (blob defects)	88.19%	94.39%
mean Relaxed Recall (linear defects)	84.10%	90.89%
mean Relaxed Recall (blob defects)	93.23%	97.03%
Inference Time (i7 7700HQ, batch size = 16)	14.87 ms/image	19.07 ms/image
Inference Time (GTX1060 6G, batch size = 16)	2.63 ms/image	3.39 ms/image

8 Conclusion

By using deep learning technology, we have achieved much more accurate inspection of the surface defects of ring magnets, and our inspection system has been in the customer site for more than a year of production use. It has been demonstrated that the initial inspection system can effectively reduce 2 inspectors for each of our customer's production line. In addition, as compared to human inspectors, our inspection system reduced the leak rate of defects by 70%, and essentially eliminated the leakage of serious defects such as short cracks, thus significantly improved the product quality. As a result, our system has been highly recognized by our customers. This is the first time we have used deep learning technology to produce an industry-leading complex surface defect inspection system with expected initial success. However, in the entire R&D process, we have identified several issues that should be further studied and improved: (1) in order to collect the 1900 defective images used in training, we spent three months at the customer production site just to collect defective products, thanks to the fact that the occurrence frequency of all types of ring magnet defects are relatively high. But if we apply the same technology to other industrial products, we may need much more time for image acquisition, our system may need to achieve the same effectiveness with fewer training samples (2) There is a certain degree of over-fitting in the trained neural network: in the trial stage of our inspection system, we observed high false-alarm rate and a few failed attempts to find out the defective product, it is necessary to add new sample images for training, with about six months of historical records/samples to achieve stability. This suggests that we should use more means to prevent over-fitting, such as using the generative adversarial networks (GAN) to generate new training samples. (3) Due to the difficulty in image acquisition, our inspection system can only detect the two planar sides of ring magnets, and can not detect the inner and outer vertical surfaces of ring magnets, so it still can not completely replace human inspectors, we'll continue to resolve the problem and upgrade our inspection system.

References

1. Ojala, T., Pietikäinen, M., Harwood, D.: A comparative study of texture measures with classification based on featured distributions. Pattern Recogn. **29**(1), 51–596 (1996)
2. Dalal, N., Triggs, B.: Histograms of oriented gradients for human detection. In: Proceedings of IEEE International conference on Computer Vision and Pattern Recognition, pp. 886–893 (2005)
3. Asha, V., Bhajantri, N.U., Nagabhushan, P.: GLCM-based chi-square histogram distance for automatic detection of defects on patterned textures. IJCVR **2**(4), 302–313 (2011)
4. Asha, V., Bhajantri, N.U., Nagabhushan, P.: Automatic detection of texture defects using texture-periodicity and gabor wavelets. In: Venugopal, K.R., Patnaik, L.M. (eds.) ICIP 2011. CCIS, vol. 157, pp. 548–553. Springer, Heidelberg (2011). https://doi.org/10.1007/978-3-642-22786-8_69
5. Russakovsky, O., et al.: Imagenet large scale visual recognition challenge. Int. J. Comput. Vis. **115**(3), 211–252 (2015)
6. Everingham, M., Gool, L.J.V., Williams, C.K.I., Winn, J.M., Zisserman, A.: The pascal visual object classes VOC challenge. IJCV **88**(2), 303–38 (2010)
7. Long, J., Shelhamer, E., Darrell, T.: Fully convolutional networks for semantic segmentation. In: Proceedings of the IEEE Conference on Computer Vision and Pattern Recognition, pp. 3431–3440 (2015)
8. Badrinarayanan, V., Kendall, A., Cipolla, R.: Segnet: A deep convolutional encoder-decoder architecture for image segmentation. arXiv:1511.00561 (2015)
9. Chen, L.-C., Zhu, Y., Papandreou, G., Schroff, F., Adam, H.: Encoder-decoder with atrous separable convolution for semantic image segmentation. In: Ferrari, V., Hebert, M., Sminchisescu, C., Weiss, Y. (eds.) ECCV 2018. LNCS, vol. 11211, pp. 833–851. Springer, Cham (2018). https://doi.org/10.1007/978-3-030-01234-2_49
10. Peng, C., Zhang, X., Yu, G., Luo, G., Sun, J.: Large Kernel Matters– Improve Semantic Segmentation by Global Convolutional Network, arXiv:1703.02719
11. Zhang, Z., Zhang, X., Peng, C., Cheng, D., Sun, J.: ExFuse: Enhancing Feature Fusion for Semantic Segmentation, arXiv:1804.03821
12. He, T., Zhang, Z., Zhang, H., Zhang, Z., Xie, J., Li, M.: Bag of Tricks for Image Classification with Convolutional Neural Networks, arXiv:1812.01187

Author Index

Printed in the United States
By Bookmasters